LABOR UNREST IN SCRANTON

LABOR UNREST IN SCRANTON

MARGO L. AZZARELLI & MARNIE AZZARELLI

THE History PRESS

Published by The History Press
Charleston, SC
www.historypress.net

All photos are courtesy of the Lackawanna Historical Society
unless otherwise noted.

First published 2016

Manufactured in the United States

ISBN 978.1.46711.877.4

Library of Congress Control Number: 2015960006

Notice: The information in this book is true and complete to the best of our knowledge. It is offered without guarantee on the part of the authors or The History Press. The authors and The History Press disclaim all liability in connection with the use of this book.

This book is dedicated to our grandmother Susanna Rossi and Jack and Angel Azzarelli. Three lights have gone out of our lives, but our hearts and memories will be filled with the warm glow of our love for them forever!

CONTENTS

Acknowledgements 9
Introduction 11

Part 1: Bloody August 1 13
Part 2: The Plight of the Miner 47
Part 3: Voices of Labor and Capital 69
Part 4: The Great Strike That Affected a Nation 85
Part 5: The Legacy 113

Bibliography 129
Index 135
About the Authors 139

Acknowledgements

Our love and appreciation go out to our family and friends, including the furry ones. We'd like to thank everyone at The History Press/Arcadia—especially Karmen Cook for all her help and support. An author couldn't have asked for a better editor. We especially would like to thank the Lackawanna Historical Society, the Pennsylvania Anthracite Heritage Museum, Reverend Samuel Crothers Logan and Lucia Dailey for their preservation of labor history, as well as the IWW Local 570, particularly Alex Lotorto, John Christiansen, Allison Petryk, Sam Emmons, Brendan Regan, Otto Von Hanneman, Joe and Jen Bruno and Brian Fanelli. Thank you for keeping up the fight for the rights of the laboring class that began more than a century ago.

INTRODUCTION

The origin of labor unions dates back to the eighteenth century and the Industrial Revolution in Europe. Labor union history in the United States began in the nineteenth century with the founding of the National Labor Union (NLU) in 1866. Unlike today's unions, the NLU was not exclusive to a particular type of worker. And although the NLU crumbled without making significant gains in establishing workers' rights, its founding set an important precedent in our country.

Scranton was on the forefront of the labor movement and played a key role in the Industrial Revolution with the birth of the Historic Scranton Iron Furnaces in 1840. As the city's roots deepened in the mines, it gained the moniker as the Anthracite Capital of the World, and many immigrants from Wales and Ireland flocked to the area seeking jobs.

At the time the city was incorporated in 1866, the men working in the mines began to organize for higher wages and better working conditions, and they enlisted the help of the Workingmen's Benevolent Association. After the Civil War, times were hard, and the cost of living soared. Miners could no longer support their families on the wages they were earning, and labor strikes became prevalent throughout the latter part of the nineteenth century. Violent confrontations between labor and capital erupted frequently.

Two events stand out in Scranton's labor history: the Great Railroad Strike of 1877 and the 1902 Anthracite Strike. As an effect of the nation's labor unrest in 1877, a riot occurred in the city, and history was made at the corner of Lackawanna and Washington Avenues. Lives were lost and prominent men of the city were charged with murder. Though victory was not on the side of the workingman, their plight and hardships at the hand of capitalism could no longer be denied by the rest of the nation.

The riots of 1877 were only the beginning of decades of violence and strikes, all leading up to the Great Anthracite Strike of 1902, headed by labor leader John Mitchell. The strike lasted 163 days, and for the first time, the government intervened. President Theodore Roosevelt requested an Anthracite Coal Strike Commission to be formed, and its hearings began in Scranton at the Lackawanna County Courthouse in November 1902. Labor lawyer Clarence Darrow represented the coal miners and championed for the rights of the working class. Once again, Scranton played an important part in changing labor history.

John Mitchell's last resting place is locally at the Cathedral Cemetery. He wished to be buried in the city because he felt his biggest labor triumph took place in Scranton, and he is honored by the people every year on October 29 in order to keep the memory of that triumph alive.

The people of Scranton who fought for organized labor sacrificed much and received little in return from the capitalists when all they were really asking for was "a fair day's wage for a fair day's work."

1

Bloody August 1

And so it begins.

The year 1877 was one filled with violence the likes of which Scranton had never seen before in its coal region and perhaps would never see again—or so residents thought at the time. It was that summer when labor and capitalists fought their bloodiest battles, strikes broke out everywhere, lives were lost and the nation was on the verge of another revolution.

The building blocks of the city were cast in iron and set on a bedrock of anthracite coal, making Scranton a city destined to be the "Anthracite Capital of the World." As a young nation, anthracite coal was a major steppingstone to America's independence. For many years, we relied on the softer bituminous coal imported from England. But by 1877, we were exporting anthracite coal not only to England but also all over the world.

During the Civil War, coal reigned supreme, partially due to its unique involvement in the iron-making process, which enabled weapons and ammunition to be produced in larger quantities. Because coal was in such high demand, a miner could earn anywhere from \$150 to \$500 a month, a far cry from the \$25 to \$27 he was earning in 1877.

So, what happened? Where did it all go wrong? Some historians track the exact date to September 18, 1873. That very same day, Jay Cooke and Company closed its doors for good and the Panic of 1873 commenced. Cooke, a leading banker of his day, had overextended himself trying to finance the building of the Northern Pacific Railroad and ended up going bankrupt. This caused a bank panic. The nation spiraled into a long depression, and because others did not want to end up in ruin like Cooke, railroad owners began laying off workers and cutting wages. By 1876, wages had been cut by 18 percent, and the steady decline of the economy continued.

In Pennsylvania, the depression produced greater complications due to the fact that the production of both coal and iron, two out of Scranton's three main industries, had suffered the most from work hours being cut and low wages. For more than three years, miners and ironworkers throughout the anthracite region continued to do their jobs while hoping for times to get better. Unfortunately, they were hoping against hope.

On June 1, 1877, the Pennsylvania Railroad reduced wages by yet another 10 percent. This saved the corporation $1.5 million at the expense

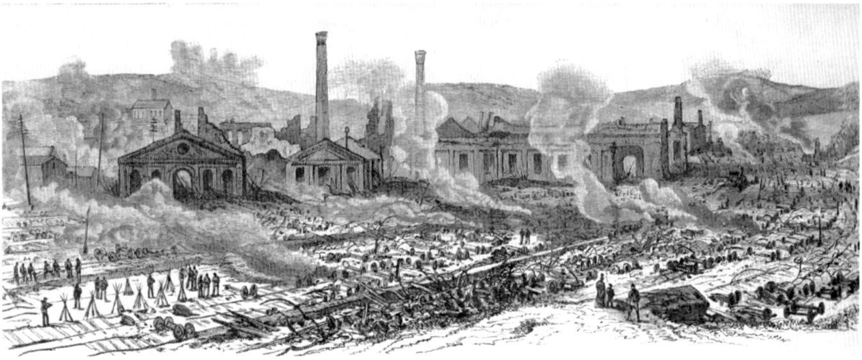

The ruins of the roundhouse and Pennsylvania car shops at Pittsburgh.

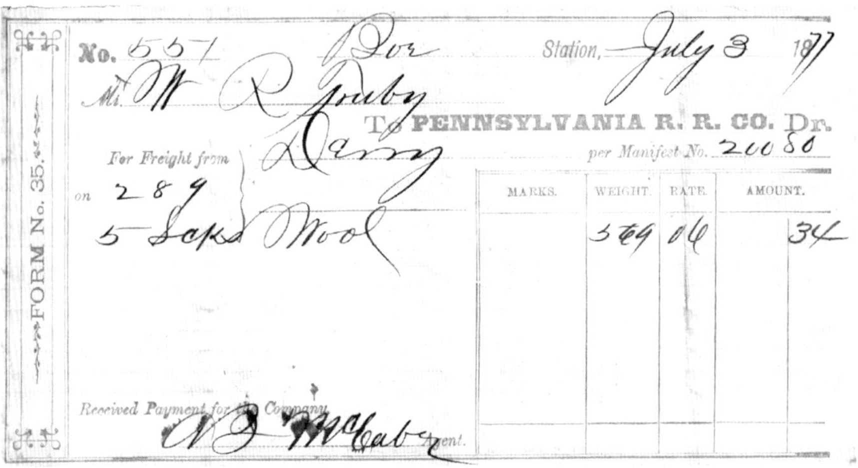

FORM No. 35.

No. 557 Station, July 3 1877

Mr. W R Gouby

To PENNSYLVANIA R. R. CO. Dr.

For Freight from per Manifest No. 2080

on 289

MARKS.	WEIGHT.	RATE.	AMOUNT.
5 Sacks Wool	569	06	34

Received Payment for the Company

Agent.

An invoice from the Pennsylvania Railroad dated July 1877. It was not long after that all trains were stopped due to the Great Railroad Strike.

of its own workers. Most considered the action no better than robbing the food right out of their own employees' mouths. Following Pennsylvania Railroad's lead, over the next forty-eight days, the major roads made their midsummer cuts, defiant of their critics and unsympathetic to the plight of their workers. Despite rumors of a strike coming from the camp of the railroad brotherhoods, the trains moved on without interruption—that is, until they ceased without a single warning.

RAILROADS STOPPED

On July 16, 1877, the trains of the Baltimore and Ohio at Martinsburg, West Virginia, were stopped and the great battle between labor and corporation commenced. The "Great Railroad Strike," as it was called, spread from the Atlantic to the Pacific. Within three days of the revolt in Martinsburg, three of the four great rail routes of commerce were blockaded; the fourth was interrupted by mobs of workmen and their sympathizers and was kept only partially opened with the help of military troops. Due to the abrupt interruption to trade and travel, a lawless spirit settled down on towns and cities. Riotous attempts were made in Buffalo, Altoona, Harrisburg and Philadelphia. But no city suffered more than Pittsburgh, Pennsylvania. The local militia was useless against the mob mainly because most of them were trainmen and many sympathized with the strikers. Pennsylvania governor John Hartranft sent troops from Philadelphia to Pittsburgh, and for three days, they battled an angry mob that seemed to grow bigger by the hour. In all, twenty-six lives were lost, and property damage was estimated to be over $6 million.

The rise of the spirit of violence as a direct result of the great strike quickly manifested itself in cities and towns everywhere, Scranton included. After learning of the riot in Pittsburgh, Scranton mayor Robert H. McKune cut his summer vacation short at Ocean Grove, New Jersey, and quickly returned to the city to find the citizens extremely worried over rumors of the local railway strike set to occur the following day. The railways in the Lackawanna and Wyoming Valleys were among the last in the state to be interrupted. Learning of the brotherhood's intentions, McKune immediately summoned his council together and found they were opposed to taking any action to protect the city should violence occur. They felt any action on their part would only agitate an already delicate situation. Mayor McKune went against their wishes and issued the following proclamation:

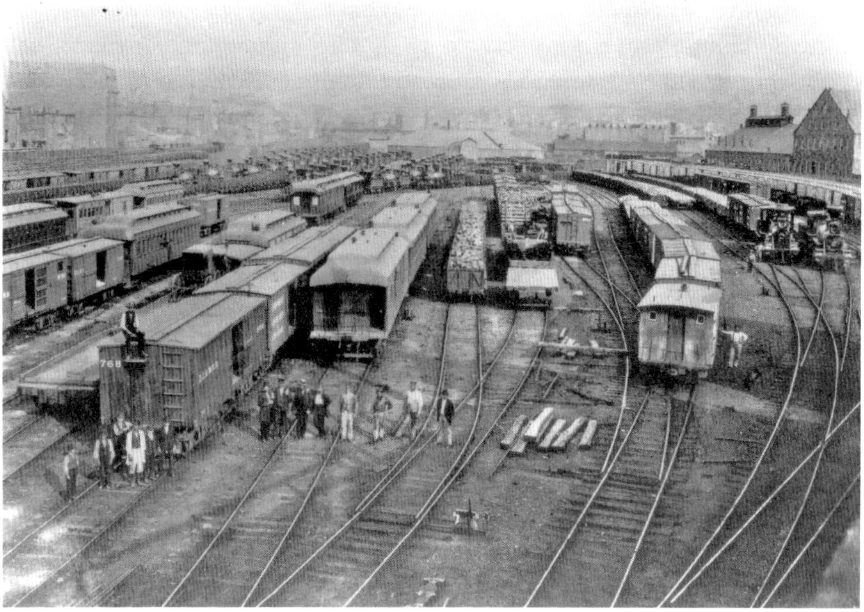

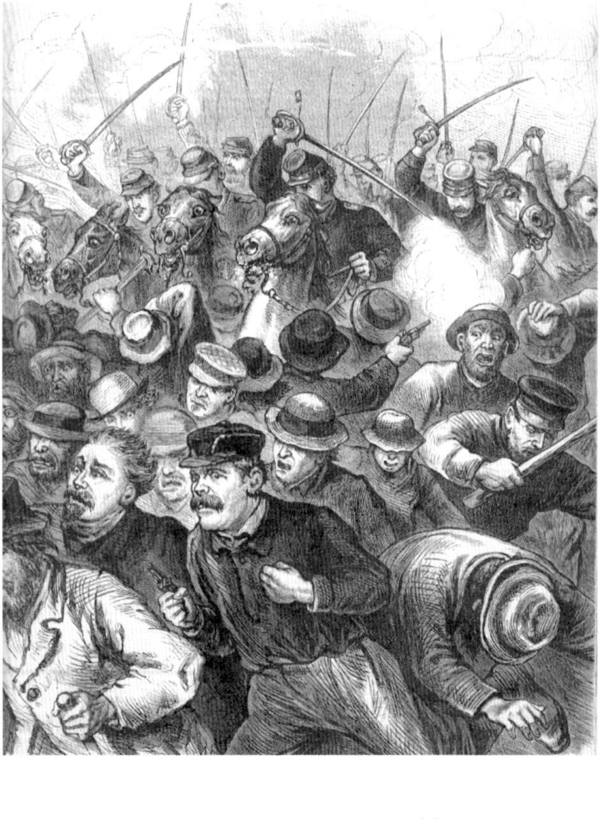

Above: The Delaware, Lackawanna and Western Railroad yard during the strike of 1877. *Courtesy of the Pennsylvania Historical and Museum Commission.*

Left: An illustration of the railroad strikes and labor riots from *Frank Leslie's Newspaper* dated August 11, 1877.

The general public opinion, as expressed to me, seems not to apprehend any violence or danger unless a too free use of liquor shall be indulged in; and at the request of committees of the workingman's organizations and others, who have called upon me this morning, requesting me to close all places where liquor is sold. I, therefore, in compliance with said request, ask of you to close your bars, and to strictly abstain from the selling of all kind of liquor for the present.

At six o'clock on the evening of July 24, after the trainmen of the Delaware, Lackawanna and Western Railway and the Delaware and Hudson Canal Company's request of the restoration of the 10 percent wage was denied, the firemen of these roads went on strike. That same day, employees of the Lackawanna Iron and Coal Company, having no connection with the railways, left the rolling mill with a big cheer and marched to the other mills, where more men joined them. For the first time since the company began, the great engines of the blast furnace and rolling mills grew silent. William Walker Scranton, manager of the Lackawanna Iron and Coal Company,

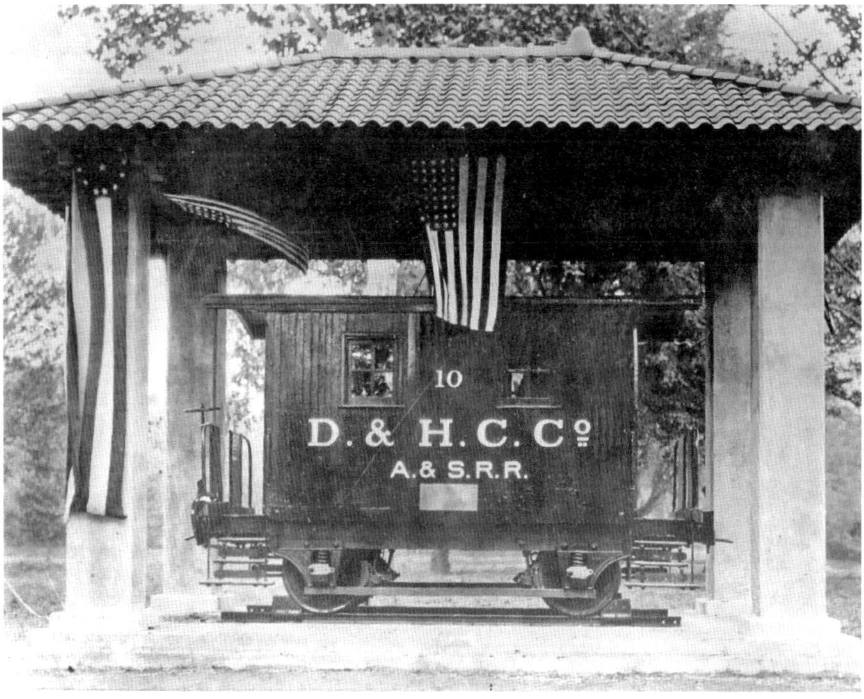

The Delaware and Hudson Canal Company dedicated the caboose to the Brotherhood of Trainmen, which was founded in 1883.

immediately demanded an explanation of his workers' conduct. He was told they could not work for the wages they were receiving, and they asked for a 25 percent reinstatement of the money that had already been cut from their pay; their request was promptly denied. The result was that one thousand of the Lackawanna Iron and Coal Company employees went on strike.

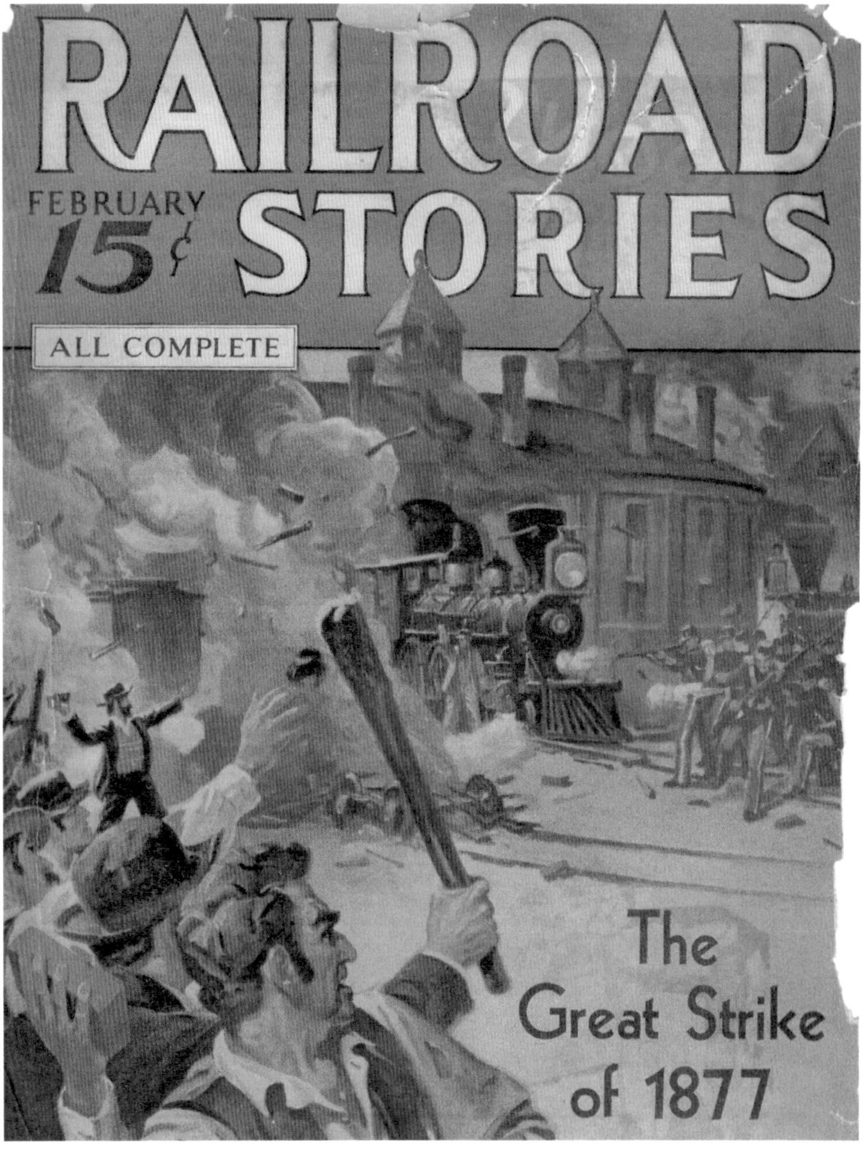

A railroad magazine depicting an image of the Great Strike of 1877 on its cover.

Locally, locomotives were taken to the yards and left in their proper places, and coal trains remained unmoved on the tracks. In less than one hour, it was all over, the strike had commenced without friction and the trainmen had retired to their homes to wait out the results.

The strike of the railway men would involve the stoppage of mining. For if the coal trains could not transport the coal to market, then mining of the coal would cease. The following day, a committee of miners waited upon William R. Storrs, the coal superintendent of the Delaware, Lackawanna and Western Railway, and requested a 25 percent advance of wages. But Storrs had no power to grant their demands, and those who could would not be able to do it in the time they gave to meet those demands. The miners' committee made its report that afternoon to a mass meeting of miners and laborers at the "Roundwoods" in Hyde Park, and the miners' strike was immediate.

People in the city were worried. As it was summer, many of their family members were vacationing, and without the trains running, they would not be able to return home. Even more worrisome, many of the troops that belonged to Scranton had left the day before under orders of General Osborne, to be used at different points in the state to maintain order. Now, Scranton was left without any military help and only eleven policemen to protect and serve a population of nearly forty thousand. The city of Scranton was suddenly cut off from all communication with the outside world, and by the evening of July 25, just a little over twenty-four hours after the first movement of the strike, every industry of the valley was stopped, with the exception of the Pennsylvania Coal Company's gravity road.

THE MAYOR'S POSSE

On the morning of July 26, the mayor issued a call to all businessmen who were willing to protect and maintain order in the city to enroll as "Special Police." He also appointed ten responsible citizens, many of whom were Civil War veterans, to act as advisors. They included W.W. Winton, Colonel F.L. Hitchcock, Austin M. Decker, Henry B. Rockwell, G. Morgan, Lewis Pughe, J.A. Price, M.W. Clark, C. Dupont Breck and Edward Merriefield. Like the city council, the group of men was divided about the need for a Special Police since the committee of miners like the Brotherhood of Railway-men had promised to preserve the peace in the city. On the day of enrollment, the mayor found two men waiting to sign up at his office door, diminishing the doubts that he had, but only temporarily, since only a few more names were added to the Special Police list. Again, many citizens felt a preparation of this undertaking would excite and anger the strikers. However, two young men who had written their names in the mayor's book felt the city needed protection. They agreed the citizens

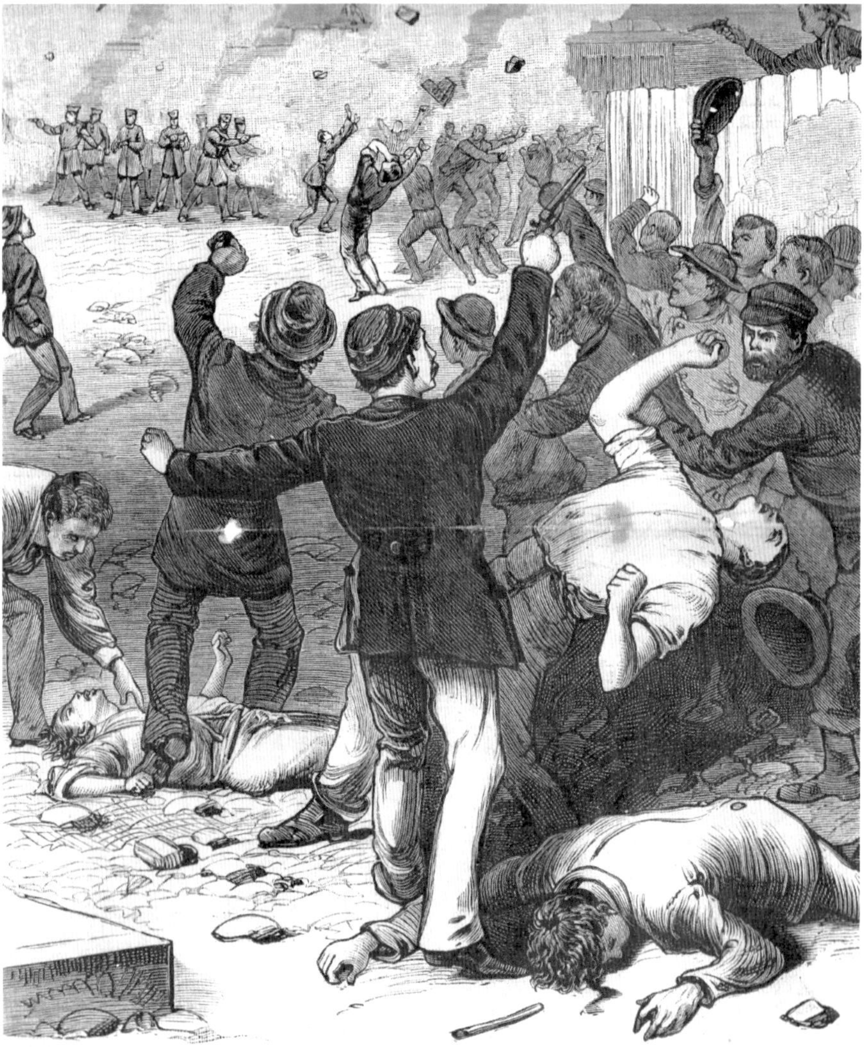

Riots broke out in Illinois and all around the nation during the summer of 1877. This sketch is of Colonel Agramontes's cavalry charging on the mob at the Halstead Viaduct in Chicago.

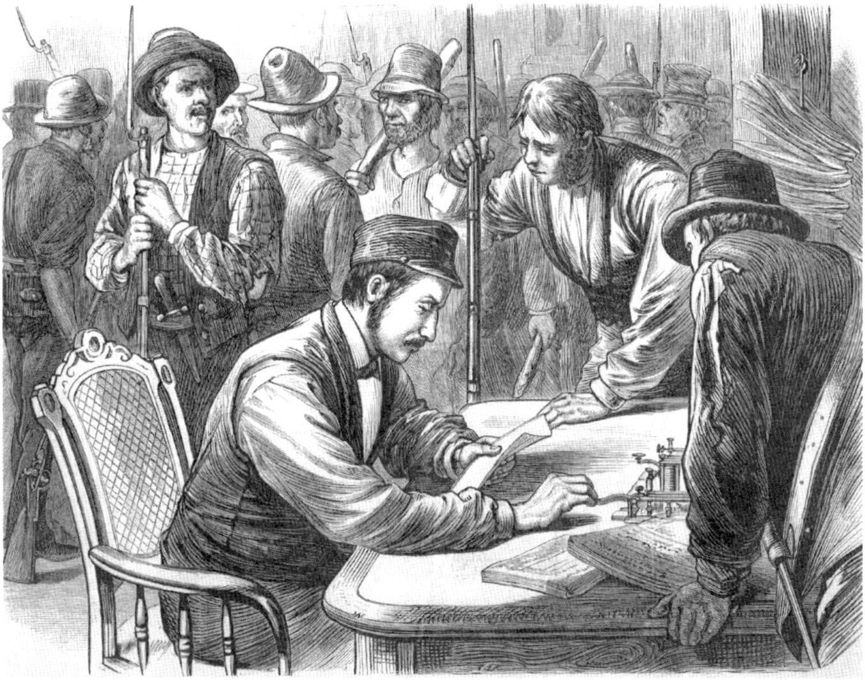

A sketch of Robert M. Ammen, leader of the Pittsburgh and Fort Wayne Railroad strike, as seen at his post directing strikers' movements.

ought to arm and be prepared to defend the city if the need should arise. But instead of a Special Police that would be overseen by the mayor, the two men set about to organize an independent company and secured signatures by quietly circulating the following paper:

> *Whereas, by a call dated July 25, 1877, the Mayor of this city has called upon the businessmen for organization; and whereas, the present state of affairs in the city and vicinity warrants a feeling of insecurity on the part of the business portion of the community; and although a creditable determination is expressed by all parties to the present conflict of interests, and while we have the fullest confidence in their good faith, still we feel that an organization, on our part, will present tangible support to their efforts in sustaining the legal authorities in preserving peace and good, order, and, will guarantee protection to property in the event of intrusion from such elements of discord as might present themselves.*
>
> *We, therefore, proffer our services as a company, to be known as the "Scranton Citizen Corps" in furtherance of the objects above set forth.*

In the end, 116 men joined the "Scranton Citizens' Corps," and by nightfall all who had enlisted gathered in the rooms of the Forest & Stream Sportsman's Club on Lackawanna Avenue. Ezra H. Ripple was nominated as captain, R.B. Merriam as first lieutenant and James E. Brown as second lieutenant. It was ordered that the company would report for duty only on the call of its own officers. Captain Ripple obtained permission from General Osborne, then commander of the National Guard in this part of the state, to collect all arms belonging to Pennsylvania and hold them in Scranton. Within three days, he and several others of the corps' members had collected 350 guns from a disbanded militia company. They were also able to obtain ammunition, and the guns were placed in W.W. Scranton's possession. In the evenings the Citizens' Corps, which later would be dubbed the mayor's posse, would meet for drill practice; all its activity was kept secret from the rest of the community so as not to incite the strikers. It was also decided that should violence break out, a signal would be given to alert the members of the corps to gather at their headquarters as quickly as possible. This signal was a specified number of taps of the bell in the First Presbyterian Church, then located on the 100 block of Washington Avenue. It is important to note that the Scranton Citizens' Corps' mission was to protect the city and the property of private citizens. Its members did not serve for pay, and they did not wish to side with the strikers or the corporations.

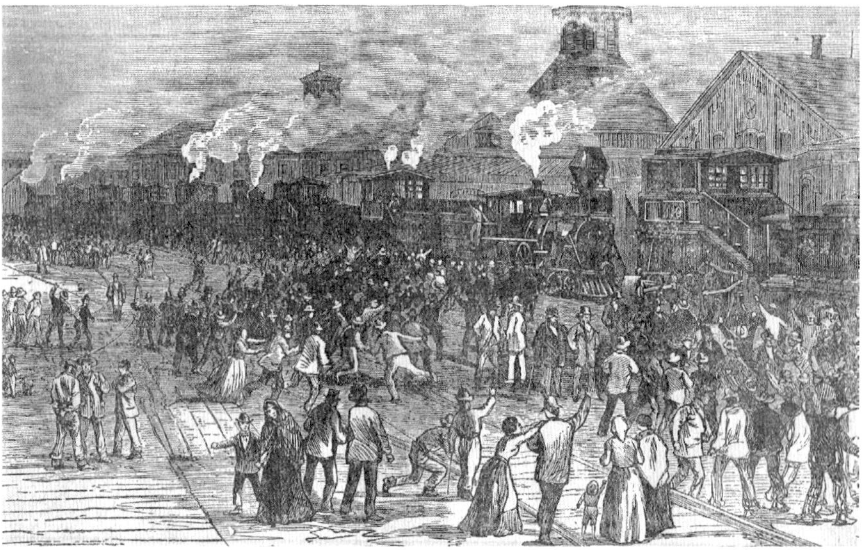

An artist's rendering of the blockaded trains in Martinsburg, West Virginia.

On July 27, Mayor McKune worked all day trying to secure a compromise between the strikers and the railway officials. Rumors that the strike was weakening began to circulate throughout the community. But all was not yet well. The next day, the twenty-eighth, striking miners demanded that the pumps be stopped at the mines. The mining engineers had left their posts at the pumps, and they were now being manned by bosses, volunteers and clerks who were not connected with the miners' association. If the pumps were stopped, the mines would be flooded, and this would bring destruction to the entire industry and leave the miners without work for at least a year. After the mayor met with the miners' committee and reasoned his points, they agreed to allow the pumping to continue in many of the mines.

There were few signs of violence in the city at this point, but strangers began to appear in the streets. The Scranton Citizens' Corps continued its drilling exercises, as taught by the members who were Civil War veterans. W.W. Scranton had his own forces as well; his men guarded the iron furnaces and the shops. Once he learned of Captain Ripple's corps, he offered the company store as headquarters for their drilling exercises.

Mayor McKune had remained on duty in his office day and night since the strike began. He had succeeded—or so he hoped—in convincing the miners that he was their friend. But that ultimately would not be the case. On the morning of the thirtieth, the committee of the Brotherhood of Trainmen met with the mayor upon his request. After a lengthy conference, they

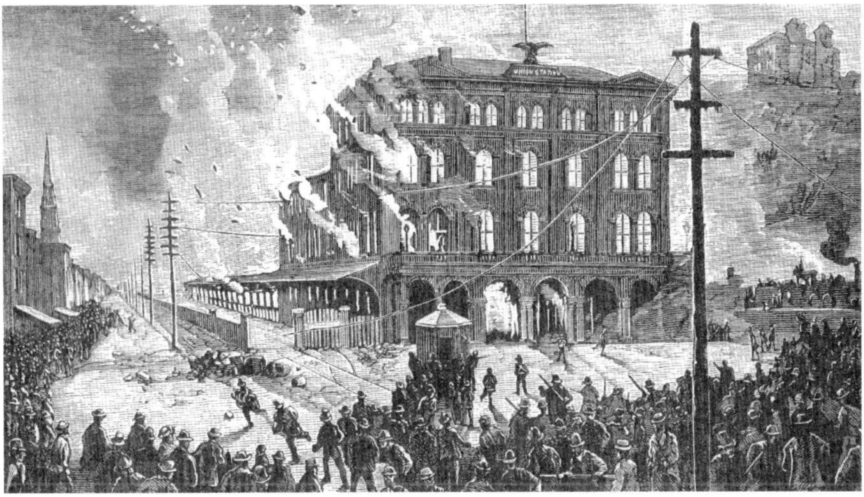

Burning of the union depot during the riot in Pittsburgh. The cost of destruction was estimated in the millions.

agreed to call a meeting of the railway strikers. That afternoon, the firemen and brakemen agreed to return to work at their old wages on the assurance that none would be dismissed for participating in the strike. A short fifteen minutes after the strike's end, "the smoke of the engines awakened from their dead sleep of eight days, began to glorify the coal yards; and ten minutes past four o'clock P.M. the first train started on its way for Northumberland."

All through the last day of the month, Mayor McKune kept in constant contact with the committee of miners trying to seek a compromise so they would return to the mines. Meanwhile, W.W. Scranton was able to lure the millworkers back to their jobs with the assurance of protection from him. At noon on the thirty-first, they fired up some of the furnaces and the men began to work. By late afternoon, a compromise between the mayor and the committee of miners was reached, but they could not accept it without the consent of the miners they represented; however, the representatives felt hopeful that they would return with a favorable answer since all they asked for would be granted, with the exception of an increase in wages. A miners' meeting was promptly called for the following day at the Roundwoods in Hyde Park.

RECIPE FOR A RIOT

The morning of August 1 dawned full of hope for the citizens of Scranton. The mayor openly spread the news that the end of the miners' and laborers' strike was close at hand. Downtown businesses all opened their doors, and the streets of the city were filled with people once again. A number of W.W. Scranton's workers had returned to the mill, foundries and machine shops and were just beginning to start their workday. Unlike Mayor McKune, William Scranton did not believe the end of the miners' strike was as imminent and continued to remain vigilant, and many of the Citizens' Corps agreed with him. Corporal Ezra Ripple, however, like McKune, felt all was well, and he returned to his office about one mile out of the downtown.

At 8:00 a.m., a crowd began to gather on the south side of the city. They came in hundreds and settled in the area near the Silkworks and not the Roundwoods, as originally stated by the committee of miners. Within an hour, the hill was covered with people. The number in attendance is estimated to have been between three and five thousand. Whether the crowd was organized by a leader, we will never know. All who were charged

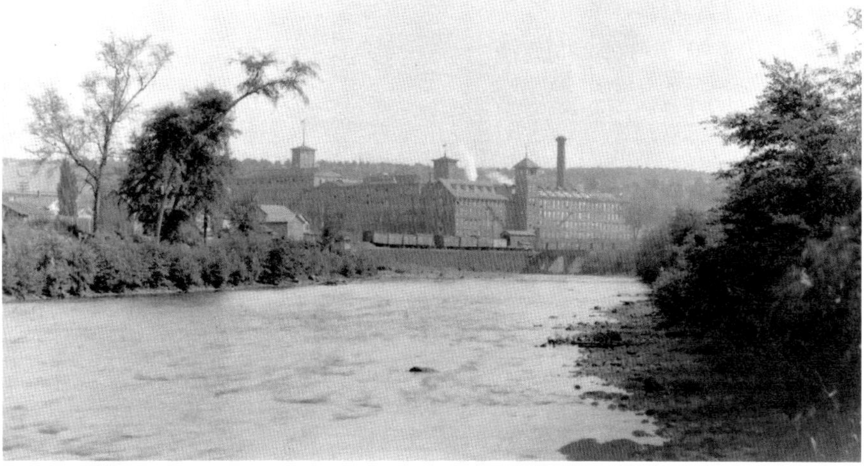

It was near the area of the Silkworks that the secret meeting of August 1 was held.

denied any connection to the meeting at the Silkworks. It was presumed the rumors of the proposal of the miners' committee to end the strike is what inaugurated the allegedly secret meeting. From what was learned in the days that followed, none of the respectable committees of miners or workers in the mills called this meeting or knew of its intention. The miners' association disowned all affiliation with the meeting, for it would have been called at the Roundwoods, where, by agreement, the miners held all their meetings. They denied it was even a meeting of the miners and said it was instead one for the lawless element that the strike had brought to town.

The men who had returned to work were called black-legs and scalawags and were seen as betrayers, and they were discussed heatedly by the crowd that gathered at the Silkworks. For several hours, more conservative men spoke with the crowd of thousands as to how to bring this strike to an end, and their opinions swayed back and forth. But then, a stranger appeared from out of the crowd and pushed his way to the front; it would be the straw that broke the camel's back. In his possession was a letter to the workingmen of the city allegedly written and signed by W.W. Scranton. The contents of the letter claimed that he would cut wages of the workingmen down to thirty-five cents a day and make them work even if it put his body

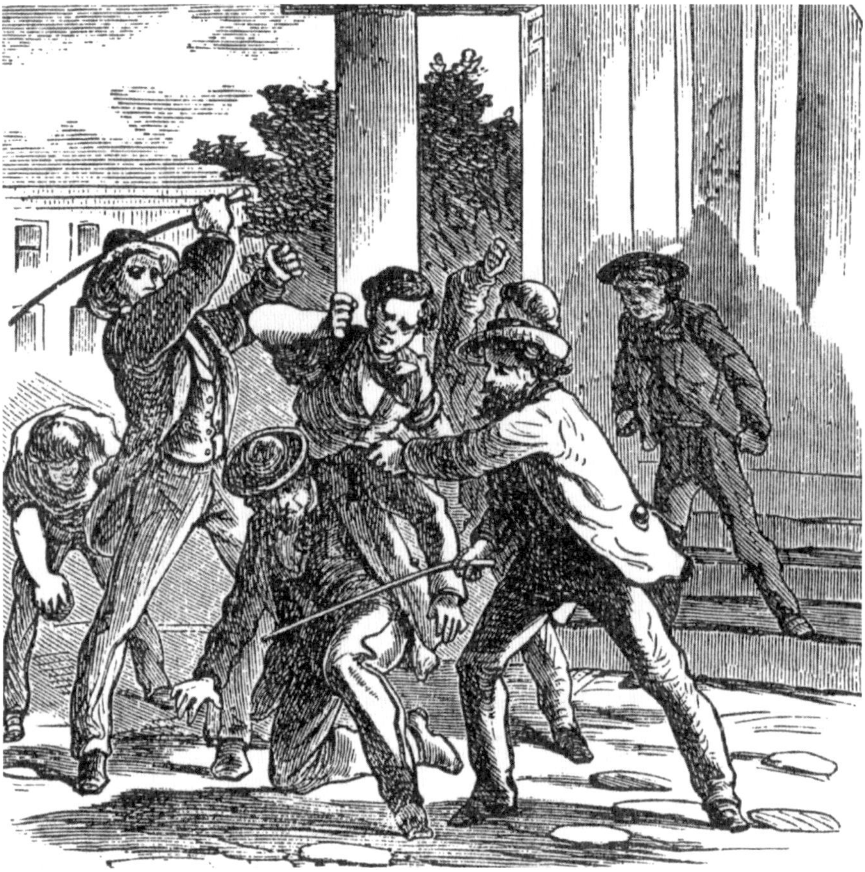

The beating of Mr. Lilly, who was considered a black-leg because he returned to his job at the car shop while others were still striking.

under a culm pile. It also went on to say that he was sorry for not being able to attend the meeting but hoped the miners would do the right thing and return to the mines. Most would later believe the letter was a forgery, but in the blinding passion of the heated moment, it was enough to turn the peaceful crowd into a riotous mob. Even normally rational men were overcome with frustration, and shouts were raised: "Go for the shops" and "clean out the black-legs."

The crowd separated and began to move in different directions. One large group headed for the blast furnaces of the Lackawanna Iron and Coal Company and another toward the Delaware, Lackawanna and Western shops on Washington Avenue. Onlookers claim they were armed with clubs, which they shook with the intent of doing harm.

Meanwhile, Mayor McKune, who had learned of the gathering crowd near the Silkworks, was not concerned, assuming it was simply a meeting of the miners, which the committee had promised to call the day before in order to bring a peaceful end to the strike. But when Arthur C. Logan, a law student and member of the Citizens' Corps, burst into the mayor's office after having witnessed the mass of excited people heading toward the city and told the mayor of their possible dangerous intentions, McKune put a plan in action. First, McKune sent young Logan to his signal post at the bell of the First Presbyterian Church and instructed him to wait for orders to sound the alarm.

The large size of the crowd less than a mile from the downtown gave others notice of imminent danger, and they began to report their concerns to the mayor's office as well. Arthur Logan and his brother Harry had strict orders to strike the alarm only upon request of an officer. Captain Ripple was at his office and could not be reached. Lieutenant Merriam and Second Lieutenant Brown could not be located either.

Mr. Scranton was notified at the First National Bank that the mob was ascending upon the city and driving workmen (black-legs) from the shops.

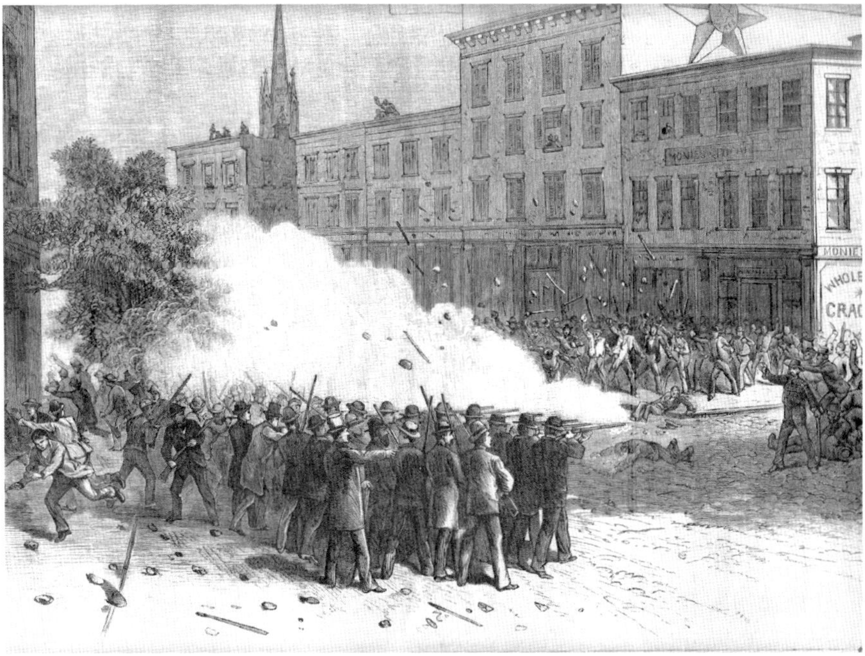

A drawing of the August 1 labor conflict between miners and the Scranton Citizens' Corps at the intersection of Lackawanna and Washington Avenues.

With the absence of the officers and the gathering of the Citizens' Corps at the company store, he sent notice for the alarm to be sounded, but it was not a legitimate order because Scranton was not an officer. As more of the members of the Citizens' Corps gathered at the company store, Mr. Scranton made a speech, advising the men to shoot low and to shoot to kill if they shot at all. He told them where to aim and implored them to stand with him to the end, fearing nothing. By this time, Colonel Hitchcock had arrived with instructions from the mayor to await additional orders and opposed Scranton's aggressiveness, making an already volatile situation all the more dangerous. As this matter was being discussed, orders came from the mayor's

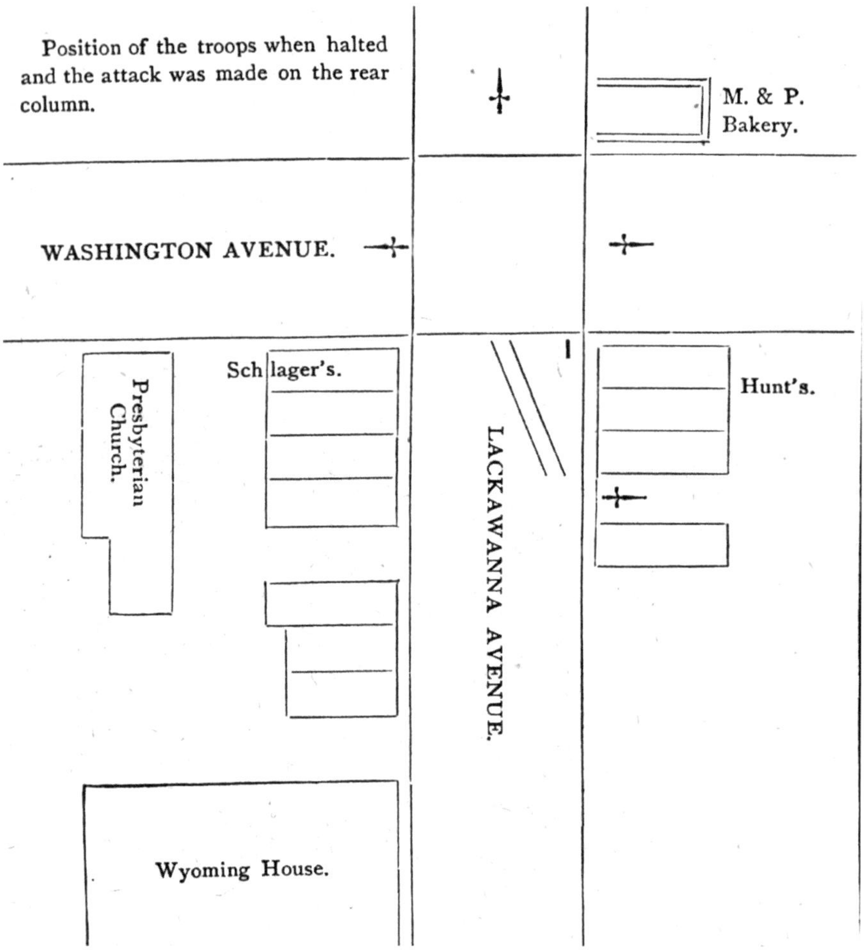

Diagram 1 illustrates the position of the column of men when halted by the crowd and when the attack was made upon them.

office for the Citizens' Corps to assemble. The men fell immediately into line armed with their guns at their sides, ready for action.

Two columns of men were formed. Twenty-four of them were enrolled members of the Citizens' Corps, recognized by the mayor as Special Police, and twenty-five of the men were employees of the Lackawanna Iron and Coal Company who would be led by W.W. Scranton. First sergeant of the Citizens' Corps, Daniel Bartholomew, faced his column of twenty-four men down Lackawanna Avenue and gave the order to march.

Mayor McKune was on his way to meet the crowd of citizens; he stopped at the office of the Honorable John Handley and asked for him to join him but was surprised when Handley declined. McKune thought the judge who upheld the law would want to help protect the city and its citizens from the impending danger. McKune hastened on alone, passing silent watchers on his way down Washington Avenue. The mayor caught sight of Reverend Father M.H. Dunn, a Roman Catholic priest; thinking the man of the cloth might be helpful in defusing the excitement, McKune took him by the arm and asked him to join him. The priest promptly consented, and within minutes, the men were confronted with the furious crowd heading toward the intersection of Lackawanna and Washington Avenues. The mayor shouted to those in front to stand back. For a moment, the people obeyed, until a large, intimidating man dressed in a black duster who seemed to take the role of their leader pushed his way to the front and yelled, "Who is this stopping the people?" Someone answered, "The priest, Father Dunn." And someone said, "It is the mayor." He immediately shouted, "Kill him!"

The mayor was struck by the man in the duster by either his fist or some kind of weapon—reports differ. The harsh blow fractured McKune's jaw, and he staggered. Another blow brought him to his knees, bringing the priest with him. Father Dunn's shouts stopped the crowd long enough for him to help McKune to his feet. The mayor, with blood running from his mouth, was bustled to the intersection of Lackawanna and Washington Avenues, where they met the two columns of men, Scranton's employees and the Citizens' Corps. According to newspaper reports, no shots were fired by either Scranton's group of men or the Citizens' Corps until the mob began to attack them with stones and clubs, but those reports would later be disputed.

Seeing no other recourse, the mayor threw up his hands, waved the bloody handkerchief he had wiped his mouth with and shouted, "Fire, boys!"

Shots were fired; bullets flew, penetrating the building of Monie and Pugh's Bakery on the corner of Lackawanna and Washington Avenues, where many onlookers had taken shelter. When the first of the mob fell,

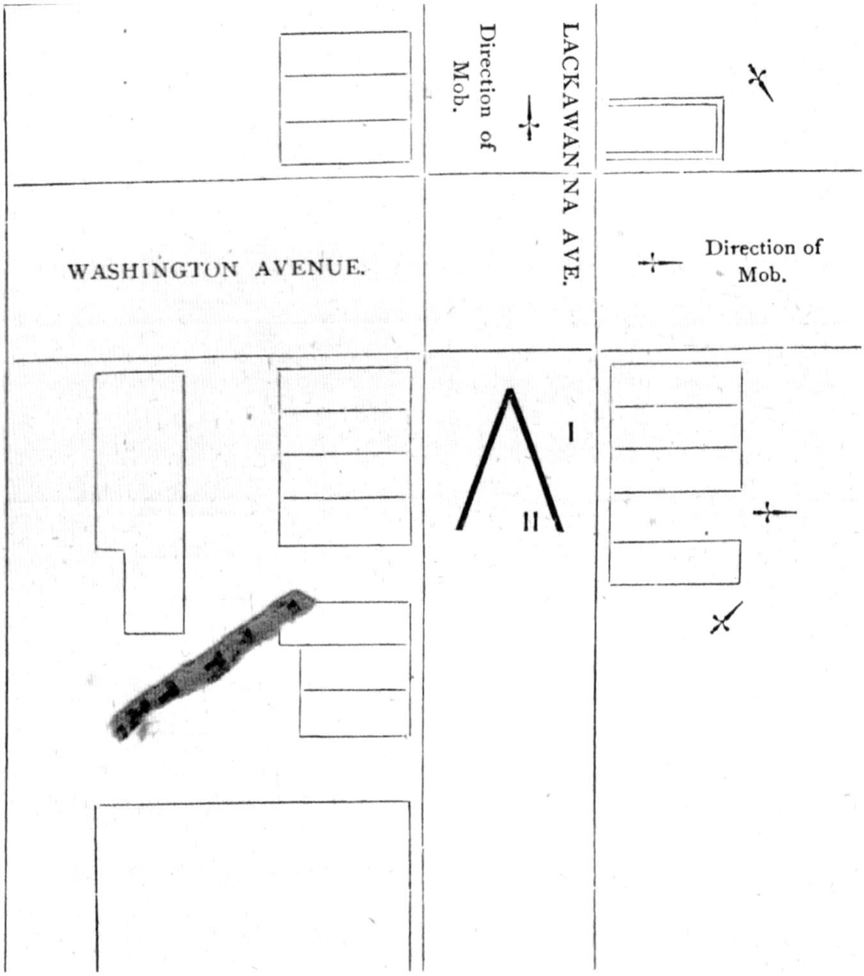

Diagram 2 shows the general position of the column of men when the attack began.

panic began to seize the crowd, and a stampede began at once. Within three minutes, the crowd dispersed and the riot came to an end. Four men lay dying or dead on Lackawanna Avenue.

Patrick Langan, who, reports claimed, was said to be the leader wearing the duster, was shot in the stomach and died instantly. Twenty-two-year-old Charles Dunleavy, who had been downtown to pick up medicine for his mother, had his skull literally torn off in front of Hunt Brothers Store on the 400 block of Lackawanna Avenue. Patrick Lane of the Bellevue area left a wife and five children, and Steven Phillips died six days later from wounds

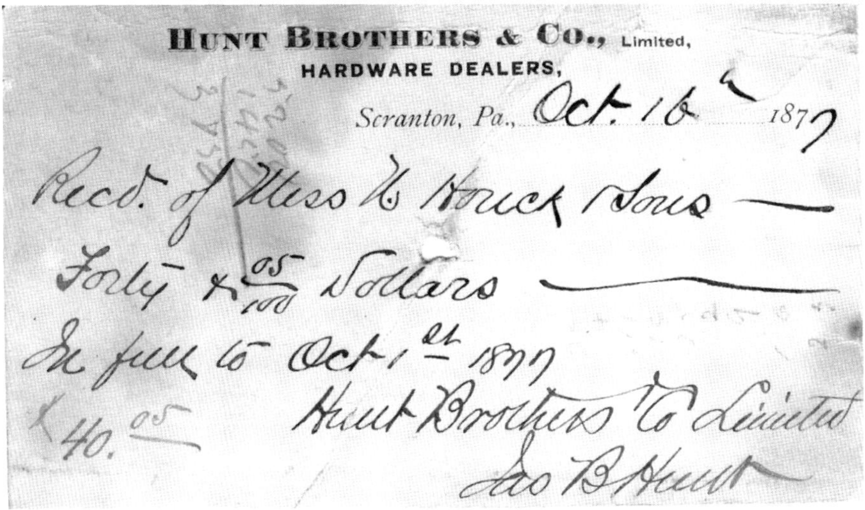
HUNT BROTHERS & CO., Limited,
HARDWARE DEALERS,
Scranton, Pa., Oct. 16th 1877
Rec'd. of Mess W. Houck & Sons —
Forty & 05/100 Dollars —
In full to Oct. 1st 1877
$40.05
Hunt Brothers Co. Limited
Geo B Hunt

Hunt Brothers Hardware was located on the 400 block of Lackawanna Avenue; Charles Dunleavy was killed in front of the store. Today, a historical marker is on the site memorializing the men who perished during the riot.

he had sustained. He resided in the Chutes at the upper end of the city. Two members of the Scranton Citizens' Corps were wounded, neither mortally. As for the number of the wounded in the mob, no one would ever know for certain. To confess you were among the wounded gave evidence of your involvement in the mob.

At this time in the city lived an African American man of marked piety who ran an express wagon to earn a living. He was known by everyone in the community for his honesty and politeness. Captain Ripple, who had joined the Citizens' Corps near the end of the confrontation, had just completed the mayor's orders to close the business houses and clear the streets when he caught a glimpse of this man and his horse. With him was a group of friends of the dead men, whose bodies were still lying at the four corners of the street. They lifted the bodies of the victims and placed them in the back of the man's wagon. When asked the cost of his services, he replied, "Nothing." He "should be happy to always serve them under circumstances like these."

With that, he tipped his hat, gave notice to his horse and took his leave with the remains in the back of his wagon, leaving the Citizens' Corps and the wounded mayor in possession of the city, upon which had fallen an eerie silence and a painful apprehension of what was yet to come.

THE AFTERMATH

The following letter was sent from W.W. Scranton, president of the Lackawanna Iron and Coal Company, the day after the riot to thank his friends for their support:

> *August 2, 1877*
> *Dear Sir,*
>
> *I have the favor of the 1st...you will thank Mr. Taylor and the other gentlemen most heartily for their kind expressions. The paper and dispatches will have posted you as to our actions of yesterday. The troops arrived this morning, and a great fright has been lifted from our minds. Our treatment by the local force has been simply infamous.*
>
> *Yours Truly,*
> *W.W. Scranton*

On the morning of August 2, the First Division of the National Guard of Pennsylvania, under command of Major General Robert M. Brinton, arrived, three thousand strong. By noon, Governor Hartranft, along with Major General Huidekopper and his company of eight hundred men, joined them. Their arrival brought a feeling of relief to the entire community, and the city of Scranton was under martial law.

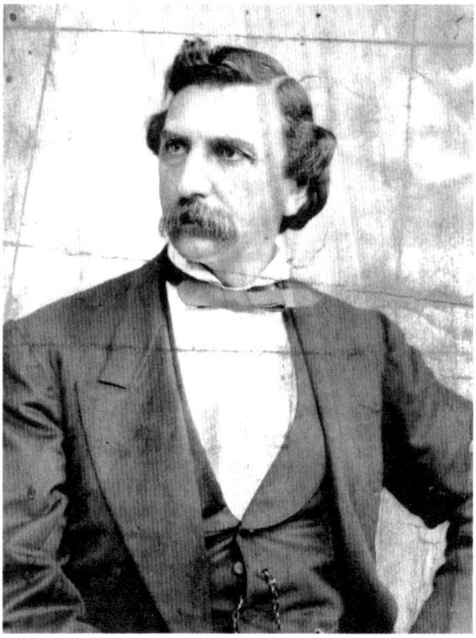

Pennsylvania governor John F. Hartranft was often criticized for sympathizing with labor.

As the smoke of the battle fought on Lackawanna Avenue began to clear, the question on everyone's lips was whether there really had been a riot. Indeed, if the answer was yes, very few in the city believed local coal miners had anything to do with the violent events of

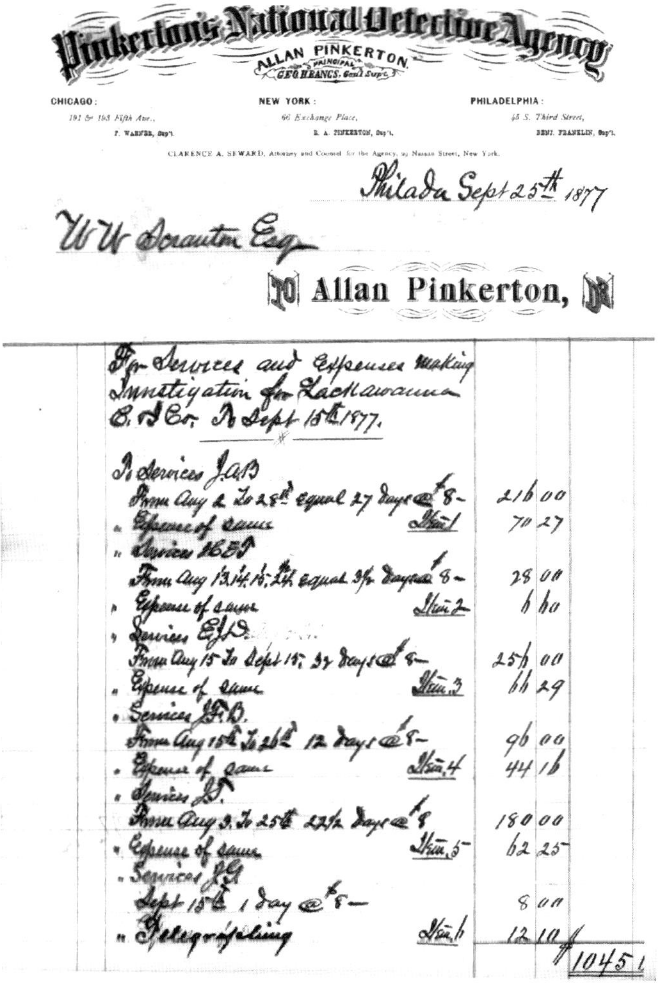

Pinkerton's National Detective Agency

ALLAN PINKERTON, PRINCIPAL.

GEO. H. BANGS, Gen'l Sup't.

CHICAGO: 191 & 193 Fifth Ave., F. WARNER, Sup't.

NEW YORK: 66 Exchange Place, R. A. PINKERTON, Sup't.

PHILADELPHIA: 45 S. Third Street, BENJ. FRANKLIN, Sup't.

CLARENCE A. SEWARD, Attorney and Counsel for the Agency, 29 Nassau Street, New York.

Philada Sept 25th 1877

W W Scranton Esq

To Allan Pinkerton, Dr.

For Services and Expenses making Investigation for Lackawanna C. & I Co. To Sept 15th 1877.

To Services J.A.B.		
From Aug 2 To 28th equal 27 days @ $8 –		216 00
" Expenses of same	Item 1	70 27
" Services H.E.S.		
From Aug 13.14.15.24 equal 3½ days @ $8 –		28 00
" Expenses of same	Item 2	6 60
" Services E.J.D.		
From Aug 15 To Sept 15. 32 days @ $8 –		256 00
" Expenses of same	Item 3	66 29
" Services J.F.D.		
From Aug 15th To 26th 12 days @ $8 –		96 00
" Expenses of same	Item 4	44 16
" Services J.D.		
From Aug 3. To 25th 22½ days @ $8		180 00
" Expenses of same	Item 5	62 25
" Services J.G.		
Sept 15th 1 day @ $8 –		8 00
" Telegraphing	Item 6	12 10
		$1045 1

Pictured is a report from the famed Pinkerton Detective Agency shortly after the riot. W.W. Scranton hired the Pinkertons to shadow ironworkers and disgruntled miners who had led the strike. The detectives tracked unhappy workers to meetings in Carbondale, where allegedly a "coffin notice" was issued to assassinate W.W. Scranton, but it was never proven or carried out.

August 1. And by the same token, there were those who believed the Scranton Citizens' Corps and W.W. Scranton's men were too hasty in firing upon the mob. For that reason, the mayor's posse became marked men.

Colonel Ezra Ripple, captain of the Scranton Citizens' Corps, described the feeling and spirit that prevailed in the days following the horrific event:

The boys of the firing squad and members of the Citizen's Corps, had hardly been relieved from immediate duty by the arrival of General Britton and his command when we had to answer at the bar of public opinion, for what we thought had been both courageously and patriotically done. We had not returned to our homes after weary night-watch, before we found there was a current of public opinion setting hard against us. All over the streets the question was being discussed as to whether there had been a mob. Many fearful souls, who for the week preceding the riot scarcely dared recognize one [of] *the Citizen's Corp*[s] *on the street, for fear he might be considered one of them, and thereby become a marked man; and who, immediately after the suppression of the riot, under the impulse of their relieved feelings, were loudest in their praise of the firing party, now as suddenly changed front again, and charged the boys with hastily yielding to the impressions and cruel demands of Mr. Scranton, which they assumed led to firing upon what they called helpless and harmless people. The whole matter began to assume very serious aspects in the company itself. The members of Corps who had not been notified until the mob had been dispersed began to feel happy that they had escaped the responsibility of the shooting and some of the members of the firing squad became so troubled that they tried to have it understood that they had not been present. Others let everyone know they had not fired their guns. Those of us who felt the responsibility in the case became perplexed and amazed. We were told that* [it] *would not be safe for us to walk the streets, for we were marked men and if we had friends, they were apparently few and we did not know where to find them. I cannot express the comfort it gave us to find here and there a man with a real backbone, who was not afraid to give us assurance of an intention to stand by us.*

The day after the mob, was about as trying a time for us as any we were called to meet. It was harder for us to defend ourselves than to defend the city. But the boys stuck together as well as they could, and did their duty, seeing that the saloons were closed as the mayor had ordered; and when night came, the whole company gathered at headquarters and remained together, because it was clear there was a danger to individuals who might be waylaid on the streets or get into trouble through the discussions of the crowds or be arrested at their homes and taken to some outlying ward to be given their sympathizers.

By public opinion, the shooting of the mob was charged as hasty and uncalled for. The mob itself had been a helpless body of unarmed individuals who had set out to persuade their fellow workers to their shops and refuse work until all could go back on equal ground. The Miners

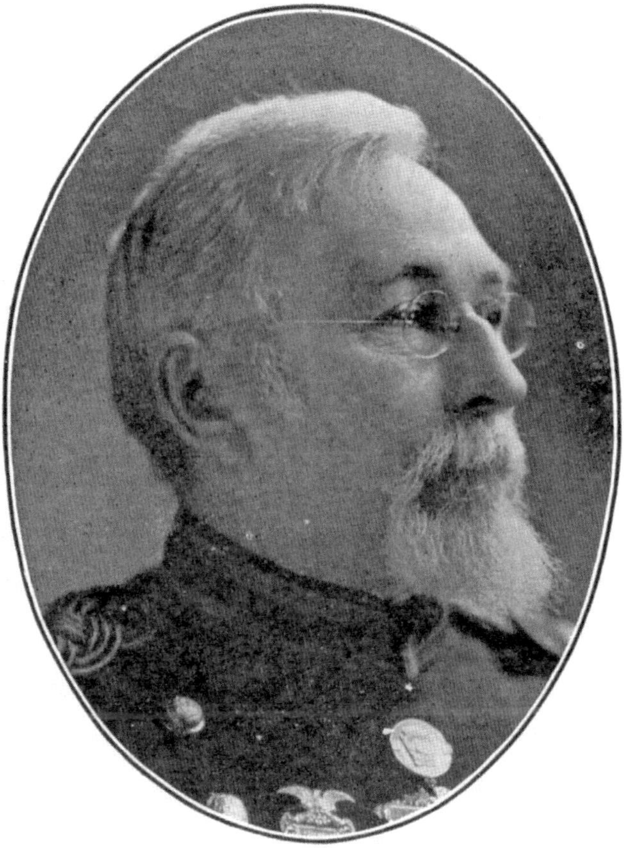

Civil War veteran and later mayor of Scranton Ezra Ripple played a key role in defending the city of Scranton.

Association denied any connection with either the mass meeting of August 1st or with the mob. This same association on August 2nd appointed a committee to prosecute the men who fired upon the mob. Patrick Mahon, an alderman of the 6th Ward had appointed himself coroner and proposed to hold an inquest of the dead men who had yet been buried.

On August 8, a charge of murder in the first degree was brought against twenty-two of the mayor's posse. The names of the accused are as follows:

W.W. Scranton, Wm.W. Peterson, Wm. F. Kiesel, L.C. Bortree, C.W. McKinney, Chas. E. Chittenden, Wharten Dickinson, Ezra H. Ripple,

> *T.F. Hunt, John O. Stanton, F.L. Hitchcock, H.A. Knapp, J.C. Highriter, J.A. Linen, M.D. Smith, Jefferson Roesler, C.S. Burr, J.E. Brown, E.D.C. Mattes, W.D. Manness, R.O. Manness, Arja Williams, George S. Throop, W.H. Storrs, W. McMiller, W.K. Logan, J.C. Highfield, George H. Ives, J.G. Lyshon, George H. Maddocks, C.H. Lindsay, E.J. Dimmick, W.B. Henwood, Daniel Bartholmew, E.L. Fuller, Enos T. Hall, John B. Cust, Curtis W. Doud, H.R. Madison, C.H. Swift, Rudolph Bensley, H. Webrum, George F. Barnard, Samuel H. Stevens, Edward H. Lynde, Marshall J. Moore Jr., Denning R. Haight, F. Franschild, John Hoffman, William M. Ringler, John M. Rose, John Hennecke.*

As soon as their $3,000 bail was posted and paid, the prisoners were released and returned to their homes. The list of men accused did not include all the men who were involved in the shootings of August 1, and it did include many who were charged as participants only after the fact. If all who had joined the Citizens' Corps a few minutes after the mob was fired on had been arrested, neither the courthouse nor the jail could have accommodated the prisoners.

It wasn't until November 26 that Judge Garrick M. Harding called the case. C.C. Rice and Cornelius Smith, Esq., were employed to assist the prosecution, and the Honorable Stanley Woodward, W.G. Ward and H.W. Palmer served the defense. The trial hinged on the question of whether there really was a riot. For the prosecution, Mr. Smith presented the rights of the workmen to meet and retire from their meeting without any interference and denied there being a mob in Scranton at the time the men were shot. Hence, the shooting could not be justified. Twenty-two witnesses had been subpoenaed for the prosecution, but only six responded. The defense was able to present to the jury twenty-four witnesses, who included men from all walks of life, from the mayor to laborers and cart men. In his summation for the defense, Mr. Woodward stated if any class of men who prevented or attempted to prevent men representing the same class of labor from working were guilty of riot. On the morning of November 27, after a much biased and lengthy speech from Judge Harding in favor of the defense, the jury retired at 11:30 a.m. and returned precisely a half hour later with a verdict of not guilty.

SCRANTON CITY GUARD

In the weeks following the riot, the citizens of Scranton were ready to accept and support the organization of a military guard for the city. Such a guard would provide the city's real defense against all general disturbances as long as such opposition between the corporations and employees should continue. By mid-August, more than one hundred men from all walks of life—lawyers and doctors in suits, mechanics in overalls, employees and employers—gathered at the company store to join the permanent military force. Henry Martyn Boies was the first to sign his name on the honorable list.

Of the many other cities dealing with strikes that year, Scranton was the only one able to contain the rioters without help from federal troops. Many thought that quite impressive—so much so that the small group of local deputized citizens soon grew to over two hundred, and on August 14, 1877, the Scranton City Guard was officially formed. Henry Martyn Boies, president of the Moosic Powder Company, was appointed commanding major. There would be a battalion of four companies—A, B, C and D—and they were mustered into the service of the State of Pennsylvania as part of the National Guard under the title the Scranton City Guard.

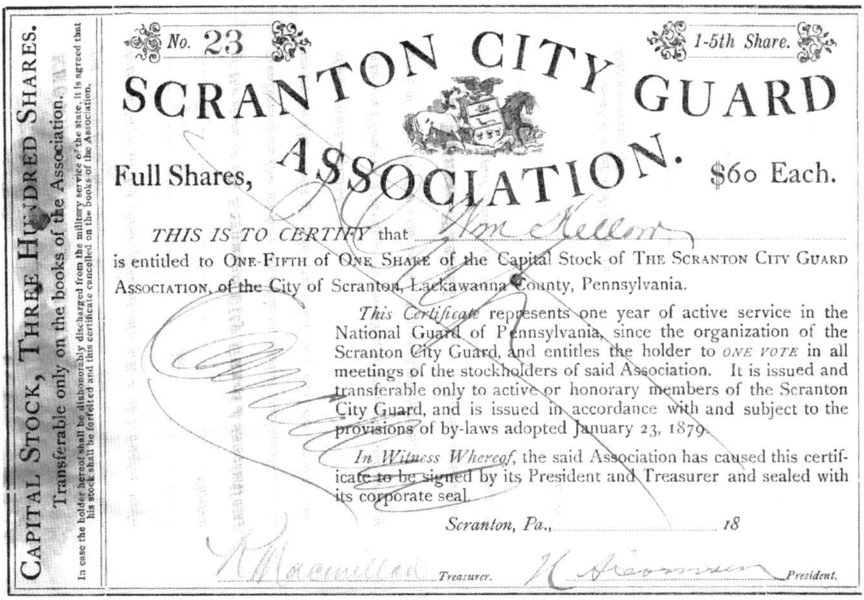

CAPITAL STOCK, THREE HUNDRED SHARES.
Transferable only on the books of the Association.
In case the holder hereof shall be dishonorably discharged from the military service of the state, it is agreed that his stock shall be forfeited and this certificate cancelled on the books of the Association.

No. 23 — 1-5th Share.

SCRANTON CITY GUARD ASSOCIATION.

Full Shares, $60 Each.

THIS IS TO CERTIFY that .... is entitled to ONE-FIFTH of ONE SHARE of the Capital Stock of THE SCRANTON CITY GUARD ASSOCIATION, of the City of Scranton, Lackawanna County, Pennsylvania.

This Certificate represents one year of active service in the National Guard of Pennsylvania, since the organization of the Scranton City Guard, and entitles the holder to *ONE VOTE* in all meetings of the stockholders of said Association. It is issued and transferable only to active or honorary members of the Scranton City Guard, and is issued in accordance with and subject to the provisions of by-laws adopted January 23, 1879.

In Witness Whereof, the said Association has caused this certificate to be signed by its President and Treasurer and sealed with its corporate seal.

Scranton, Pa., ... *18*

.... *Treasurer.* .... *President.*

A capital share of the Scranton City Guard, which was in existence from 1877 to 1878.

Officers and Members

Henry M. Boies: major commanding

STAFF OFFICERS
Frederick L. Hitchcock: first lieutenant and adjutant
Henry A. Kingsbury: captain and commissary
Nathan Y. Leet, MD: first lieutenant and assistant surgeon
James Ruthven: first lieutenant quartermaster
Samuel C. Logan, DD: captain and chaplain

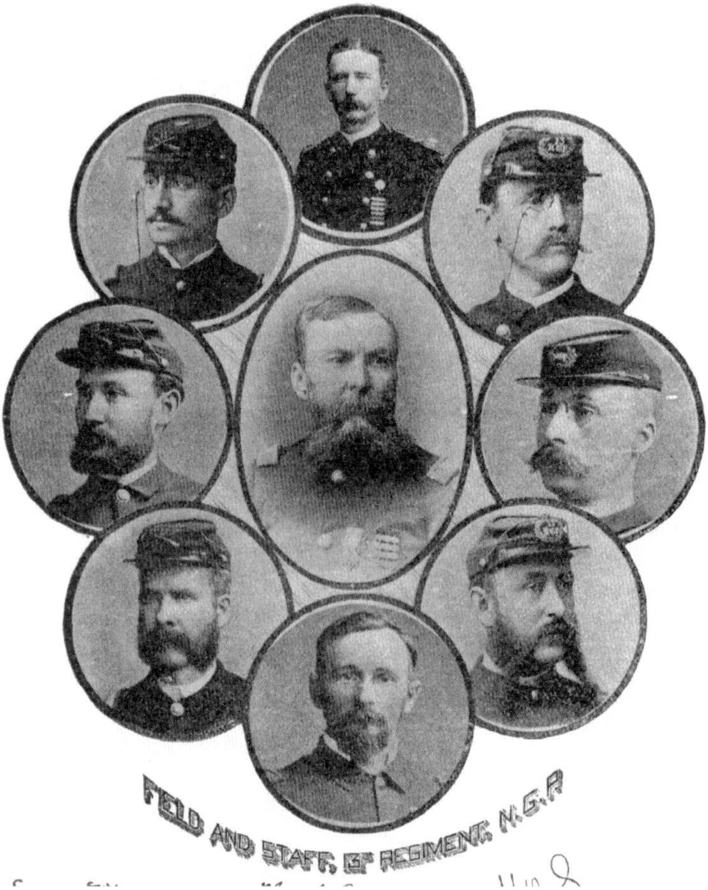

Members of the Field and Staff of the Thirteenth Regiment Pennsylvania National Guard.

NONCOMMISSIONED STAFF
Henry N. Dunnell, MD: sergeant major
Samuel G. Kerr: quartermaster sergeant
George H. Maddocks: commissary sergeant

William W. Ives: hospital steward
M.D. Smith and Charles R. Smith: principal musicians

COMPANY A
Officers
Andrew Bryson Jr.: captain
Henry A. Knap: first lieutenant
Edward J. Smith: second lieutenant

Robert Macmillan: first sergeant
H.A. Mace: second sergeant
James P. Hosie: third sergeant
John C. Highriter: fourth sergeant
Henry E. Hess: fifth sergeant

George F. Bernard: first corporal
John P. Albro: second corporal
M.J. Andrews: third corporal
S.V.D. Huntington: fourth corporal
William A. Duer: fifth corporal
Friend B. Watrous: sixth corporal
Edward S. Dolph: seventh corporal
Isaac Post: eighth corporal

COMPANY B
Officers
R.B. Merriam: captain
Daniel Bartholomew: first lieutenant
William Kellow: second lieutenant

Charles R. Fuller: first sergeant
J.D. Evans: second sergeant
H.R. Madison: third sergeant
J.N. Godshall: fourth sergeant
William J. Watts: fifth sergeant

L.C. Bortree: first corporal
John Bailey: second corporal
C.K. Swift: third corporal
L.D. Kemmerer: fourth corporal
John T. Howe: fifth corporal
H.G. Bacon: sixth corporal
Frank McFarland: seventh corporal
W.S. Millar: eighth corporal

Thomas H. Watts: company clerk

A.K. Roberts: musician
W.D. Roberts: musician
Frank G. Wolf: musician

COMPANY C
Officers
H.A. Coursen: captain
Louis A. Watres: first lieutenant
Charles E. Judson: second lieutenant

W.D. Manness: first sergeant
Edward C. Mattes: second sergeant
Edward J. Dimmick: third sergeant
J.H. Culver: fourth sergeant
C. Seward: fifth sergeant

Frank H. Clemons: first corporal
James Moir: second corporal
Charles W. Gunster: third corporal
W.B. Henwood: fourth corporal
T.F. Penman: fifth corporal
J. Vosburgh: sixth corporal
J.S. Walden: seventh corporal
W.D. Schoonover: eighth corporal

Uriah Armstrong: musician
Wesley Baptist: musician
W.L. Culver: musician

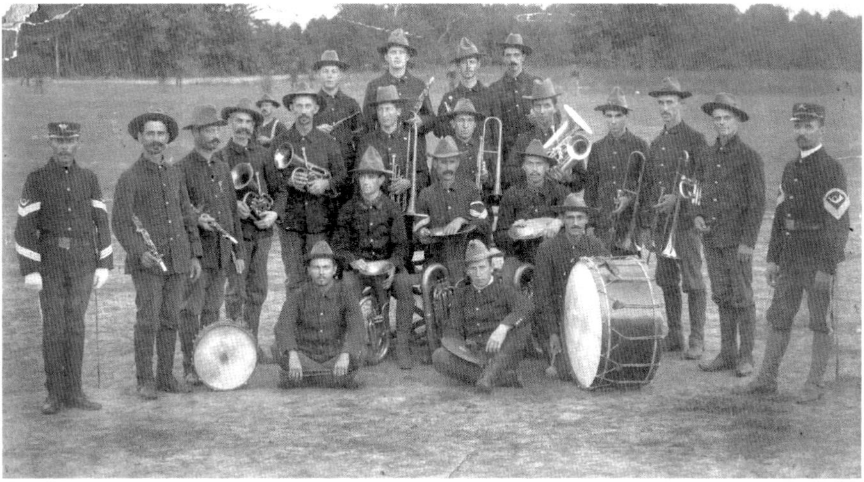

Battalion Band of the Scranton City Guard, circa 1877.

W.C. Cowles: musician
J. White: musician

COMPANY D

Officers

Ezra H. Ripple: captain
James A. Linen: first lieutenant
Samuel Hines: second lieutenant

J.L. Harding: first sergeant
Edward S. Jackson: second sergeant
George F. Millet: third sergeant
David T. Lawson: fourth sergeant
Samuel H. Stevens: fifth sergeant

E.C. Fowler: first corporal
H.T. Porter: second corporal
George F. Bentley: third corporal
Charles H. Lindsay: fourth corporal
Alexander W. Dickson: fifth corporal
H.L. Krigbaum: sixth corporal
Jacob Bryant: seventh corporal
Henry Belin Jr.: eighth corporal

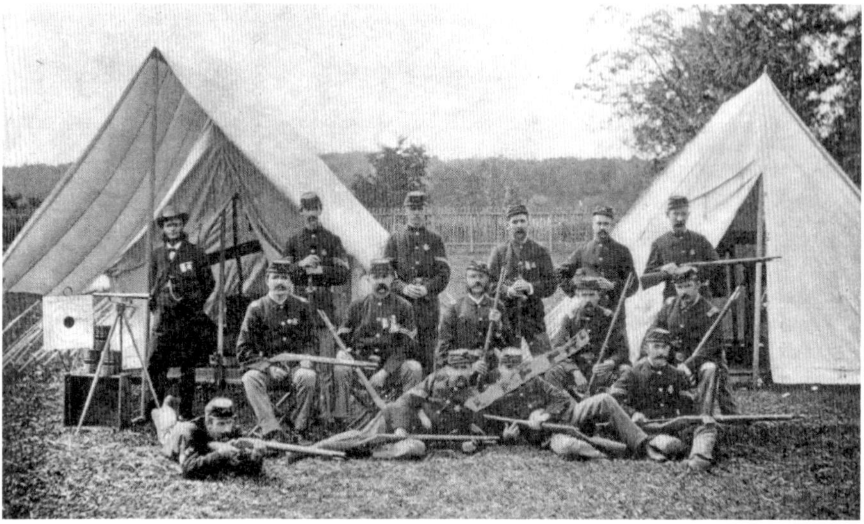

The first Rifle Team of the Thirteenth Regiment, circa 1879.

These officers and men (privates' names not listed) constituted the original organization of the Scranton City Guard. The people of Scranton were proud of their own boys; they appreciated their patriotism and the sacrifice of their time and comfort to ensure the safety of the city.

Commander Boies, along with Reverend Samuel C. Logan of the First Presbyterian Church, was chosen to secure land to build an armory. The two men purchased two lots from the Susquehanna and Wyoming Valley Railroad and Coal Company on the east side of Adams Avenue, between Linden and Mulberry Streets. The armory was completed on January 31, 1878.

The next important event in the Scranton City Guard's history was the honor of an invitation of the Wyoming Monument Committee to take part in the 100th anniversary of the massacre of Wyoming. The event was held on July 3, 1878. The battalion and its newly organized band was given the honor of escorting President Rutherford P. Hayes and his cabinet from the station to the site of the monument. At the close of the president's address, Hayes sent word to Commander Boies asking to meet all the battalion officers and men. The battalion escorted the president and his staff to the residence of Mr. Payne Pettibone, where they gave an exhibition of drill and a closing dress parade. President Hayes complimented and thanked the battalion for its excellent services, and every member received the honor of shaking hands with the president of the United States.

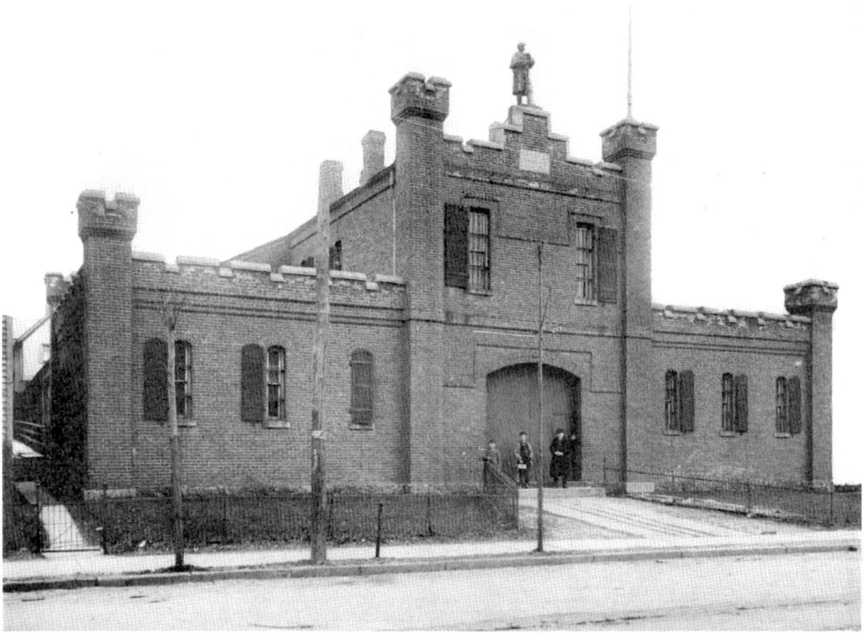

The first armory used as headquarters for the Scranton City Guard, circa 1878.

Shortly after, the legislature of 1878 passed an act reorganizing the militia of the state that consolidated battalions and companies into regiments. This act brought an end to the Scranton City Guard as a separate entity. But it was the beginning of the Thirteenth Regiment.

THE END OF THE STRIKE

At 10:00 a.m. on the morning of October 16, miners met at the Roundwoods and, by a unanimous vote, announced that they would return to the mines the very next day without the increase in wages they asked for, thus ending the bloody strike of 1877. Many have written off the "Great Strike" as a failure. Yet the *New York Times* of that day labeled it "a drawn battle": "The workmen have attracted so much attention in their grievances that future indifference to their plight would be impossible, the balance of gain is on the side of the workmen."

It took some time for life to return to normal in the city of Scranton, but it eventually did. The miners, having been advised by Judge Harding to take

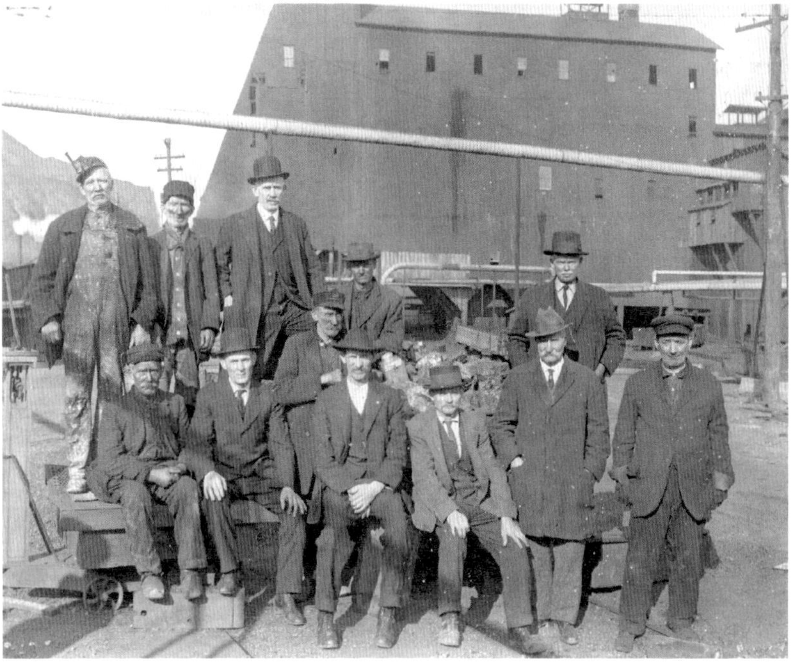

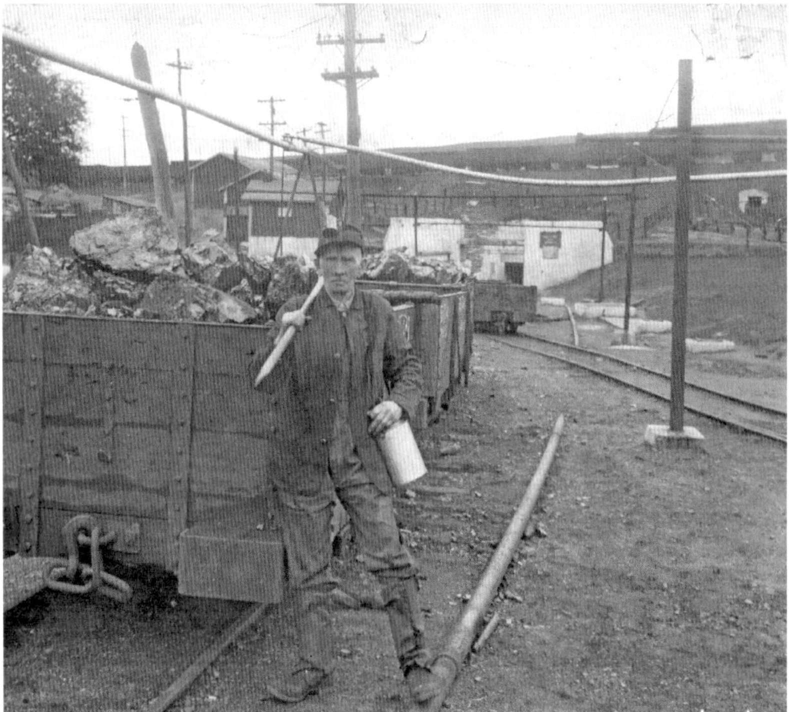

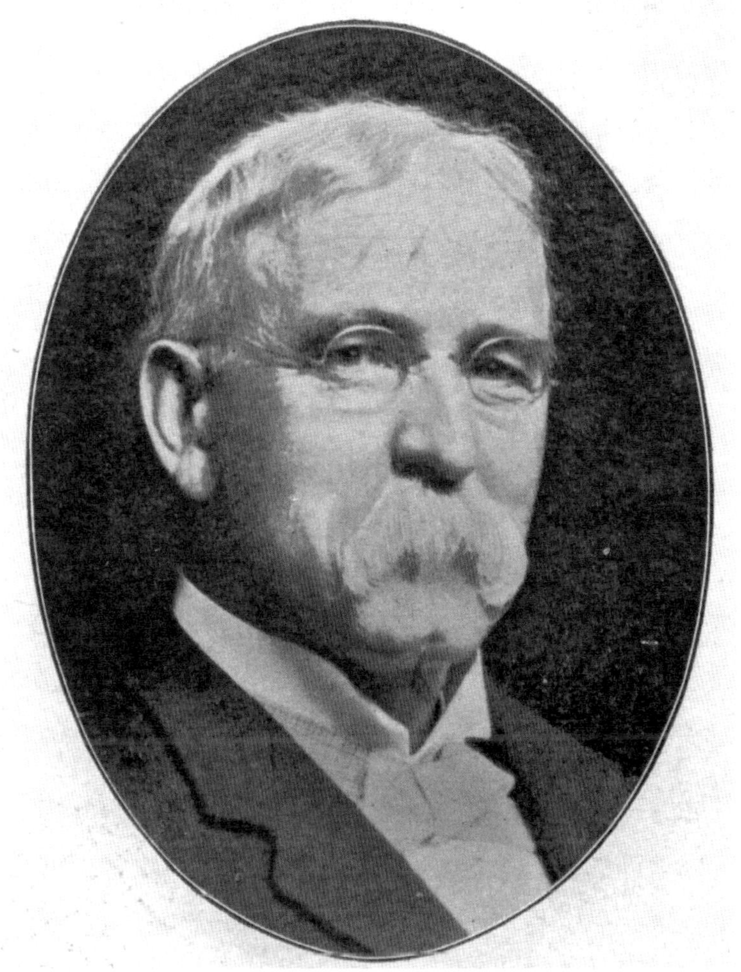

Portrait of Scranton's fifth mayor (1878–84) and leader of the Knights of Labor, Terrence V. Powderly.

Opposite, top: Governor Gifford Pinchot (front, second from right) and employees of the Marvine Colliery, circa 1930.

Opposite, bottom: Miners worked with picks, shovels and steel drills to break loose the layers of coal. Sometimes, they would have to lay on their sides to complete this task.

their grievances to the ballot box instead of resorting to violence, voted in Terrence Powderly, representing the Greenback Labor Party, as Scranton's mayor the following year. This was a definite triumph for the laboring class. Another victory was the dawn of a new county, formed on August 13, 1878. After a landslide vote, the upper end of Luzerne County became Lackawanna County. Regardless of victories and defeats, the blood of the workingman will forever stain Lackawanna Avenue, reminding us of all the sacrifices they made in the name of labor.

2

The Plight of the Miner

Coal in the United States

From the mid-nineteenth to the early twentieth century, nothing fueled the United States of America like anthracite coal. Coal power was an efficient and cost-effective way to power homes, steam locomotives and the factories that produced everyday and industrial items that built America into what it is today.

Coal was quite literally the bedrock of the nation's progress throughout the Industrial Revolution. It is estimated that in the United States alone there is enough coal to last for 2,500 years. Out of fifty states, twenty-five of them contain coal, but the largest of these fields is in the Appalachian coal area, which ranges from Alabama north to Pennsylvania and Ohio.

By the 1830s, large-scale coal mining started in Pennsylvania and other plentiful coal states. Northern railroads like the Delaware, Lackawanna & Western replaced their wood and water power because of the abundance of coal produced. During the American Civil War in the 1860s, the Union produced thirty-eight times more coal compared to the floundering Confederacy, giving the North a material advantage. After the Civil War, the demand for anthracite grew as the Industrial Revolution did, and by the 1890s, America became one of the largest coal producers in the world. Every year up until the 1910s, 750,000 coal miners of more than three dozen nationalities blasted and dug out 550 million tons of a coal. One of the largest states for this immense industry was Pennsylvania.

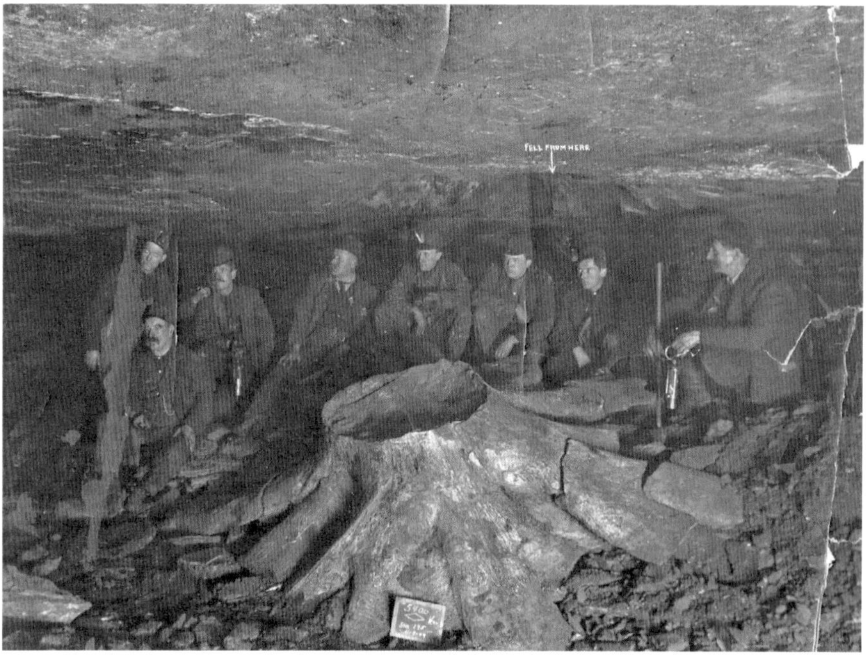

A petrified tree stump in the Diamond Mine located in Scranton, circa 1900.

The reason Pennsylvania was so important was for the large amount of anthracite coal found in the north, central and southern coal fields, which include Lackawanna, Luzerne, Columbia, Carbon, Schuylkill, Northumberland and the northeast corner of Dauphin Counties. Anthracite is the harder, slower-burning sister to bituminous coal, which is mined in states like Illinois. Anthracite was considered a more reliable source of heat and energy because it lasted longer and for the lack of ash and soot that came off it. The idea that anthracite was a clean-burning coal became so famous that the Delaware, Lackawanna & Western started creating advertisements in the early 1900s portraying a young "Gibson Girl" named Phoebe Snow, who wore an entire outfit of white and loved to travel the "Road of Anthracite" without a speck of soot on her. Even Mark Twain wrote to the DL&W in 1899 just to let it know that he wore a "white duck suit" on his trip to Elmira, New York, and that it was still white when he reached his destination.

COMING TO AMERICA

With the boom of the anthracite coal industry in the late nineteenth century, more miners and laborers were needed to meet demand. The ever-resourceful coal operators, who had to deal with a shortage of American labor that was spreading throughout the country, turned to the European immigrants who flooded the country by the millions looking for the American dream. The operators saw the influx as a new source of employees who were willing to work hard for less money than an American would. It also lessened the increasing problem of workers' strikes because, with the number of people coming to America each day, every rebellious worker was easily replaceable.

Thus, the mining of coal became a job that was predominantly done by people who came to America to find work and refuge. In 1860, the population of Scranton was 9,000, and it grew to an astonishing 35,000 by 1870. Of that population, 15,887 were foreign-born, with almost all of them working in the mines.

At that time, the majority of mine workers and laborers in the area were Welsh and Irish. It wasn't until the 1870s and 1880s that residents of countries like Poland and Italy began to immigrate to America and made their way to the

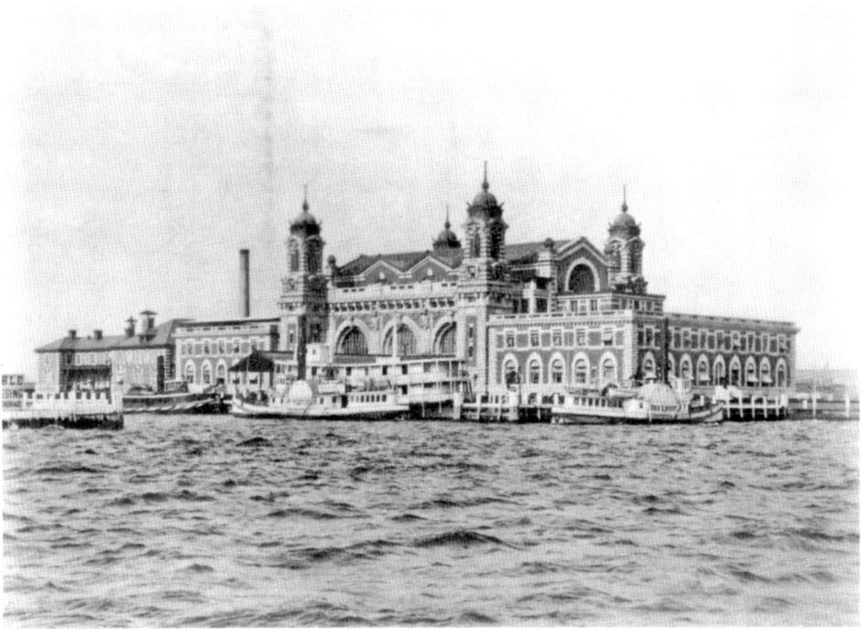

Ellis Island, where many of our ancestors came through to enter the United States.

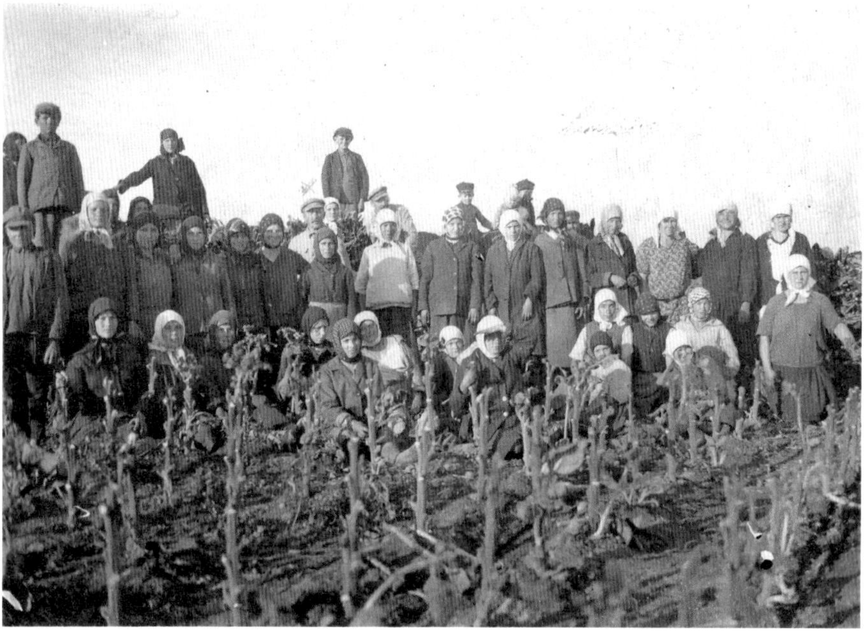

A group of Hungarian immigrants.

Pennsylvania coal mines. Out of the early Welsh and Irish immigrants, it was the Welsh who were known to be skilled workers because of their mining experience in their own country, so they usually held positions higher than the Irish, who made up more of Scranton's foreign population than the Welsh.

To an immigrant striving for the American dream of stable work and a home of his own, a job as a coal miner with the security of a house and a neighborhood populated with people from his own country seemed like one of the best ways to start out in the New World. Sadly, what these people hoped for didn't always come to fruition, and the life of a Pennsylvania miner was anything but dream like.

DOWN IN THE MINE

One of the most popular tourist destinations in Scranton, Pennsylvania, is the tour of the No. 190 slope located in McDade Park. Its popularity even reached national levels when it was mentioned on an episode of *The Office*, a TV show based in Scranton. The tour of the coal vein is an exciting

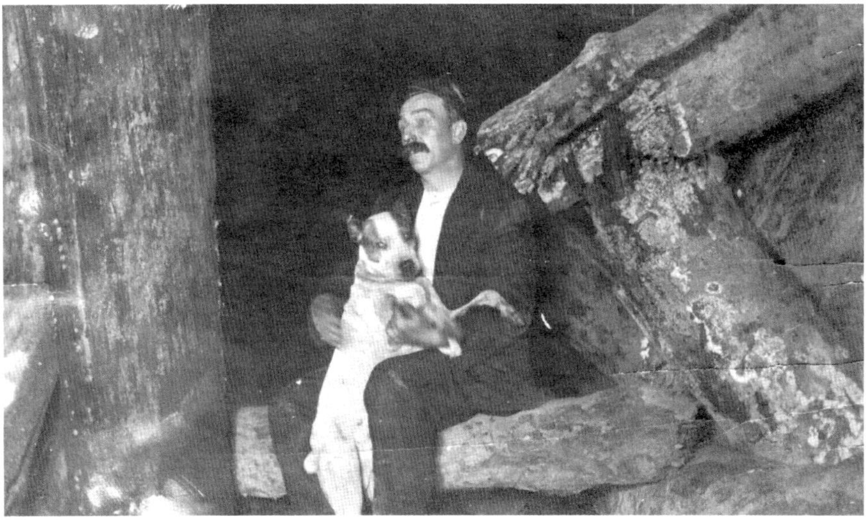

A coal miner and his best friend.

experience for most, as they ride down the slope, deep into the earth to get the experience of what it would have been like to be a coal miner in the nineteenth century.

When you make it down the slope to the mine, the first thing you notice is the cold. No matter what time of year, it is always fifty to fifty-four degrees in the mine. The next thing you may notice as you walk through the mine is the distinct smell of the dirt and damp that constantly floats through the air. The last thing you may notice—and it is only if your tour guide will turn off his lantern to show you—is how incredibly dark and noiseless it is deep down under the earth. This is what the miner, laborer, mule boy and nipper experienced every day, except for Sundays, going months seeing only a little bit of sunlight and constantly covered in dirt and dust for nine to twelve hours of work a day.

In the nineteenth and early twentieth centuries, mining was a rough and unforgiving job for both the laborers and the miners. According to Reverend John McDowell, who was once a miner himself and wrote about the lives and jobs of coal workers in 1902, there is a distinct difference between a laborer and a miner and what their respective jobs are:

> *The laborer is employed by the miner, subject to the approval of the superintendent, to load the cars with the coal which has been blasted by the miner. As a rule he is paid so much per car, and a definite number of cars*

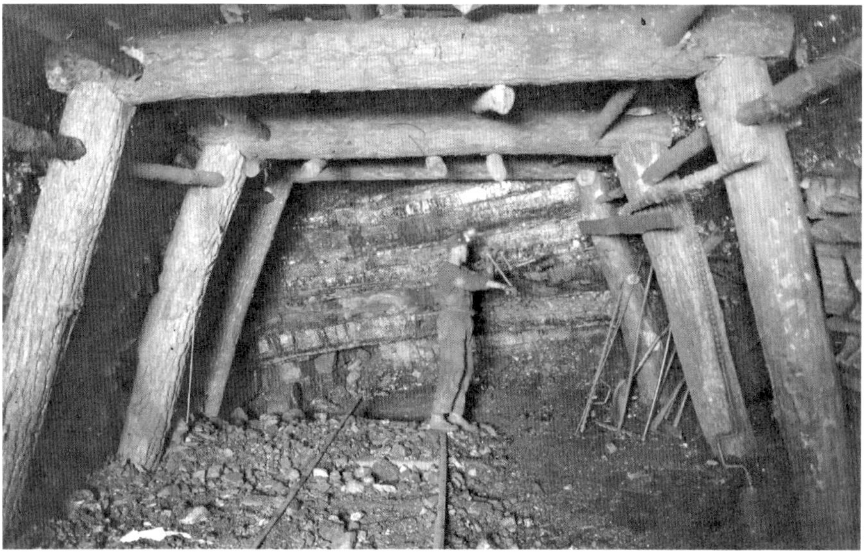

Down in a coal mine in Pennsylvania.

> *constitute a day's work—the number varying in different mines—averaging from five to seven, equaling from twelve to fifteen tons of coal. The laborer's work is often made difficult by the water and rock which are found in large quantities in coal veins.*

The miner, unlike the laborer, had more control over what was being blasted and dug from the mines and actually had a contract with the mine company:

> *He enters into a contract with the company to do a certain work at so much per car or yard. He blasts all the coal, and this involves judgment in locating the hole, skill in boring it, and care in preparing and determining the size of the shot. The number of blasts per day ranges from four to twelve, according to the size and character of the vein. He is responsible for the propping necessary to sustain the roof. According to the law of the State of Pennsylvania, the company operating the mine is obliged to furnish the miner the needed props, but the miner must place them at such places as the mine boss designates. Most of the boring is now done with hand machines.*

Besides the fact that most, if not all, of these jobs were done by hand, the workers had to buy their own tools with their own salary just to do their job properly. This equipment and tools included powder, squibs, paper, soap, oil, a

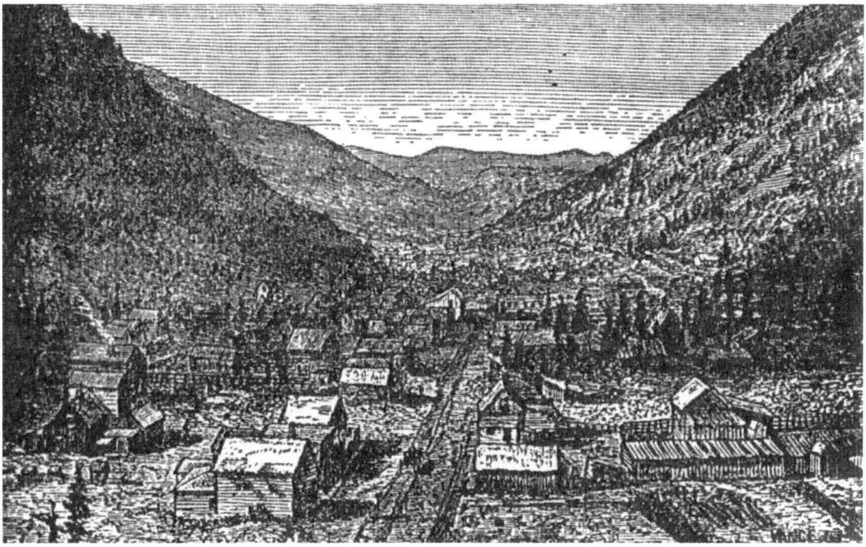

A view of the anthracite mining region in 1877.

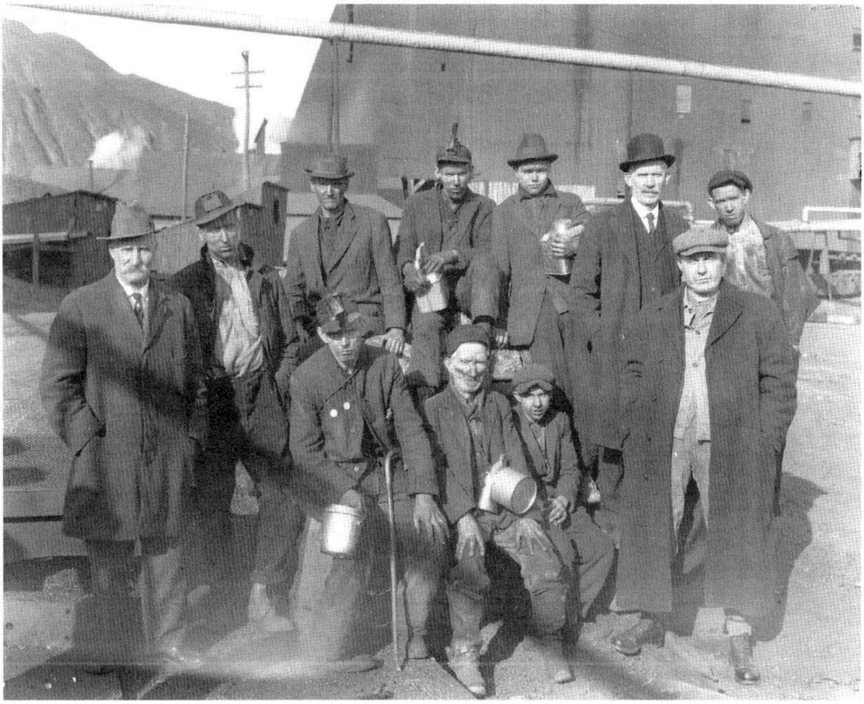

A group of coal miners pose for a photo with the mine bosses.

hand-powered drilling machine, drill, scraper, needle, blasting barrel, crowbar, pick, shovel, hammer, sledge, cartridge pin, oil can, toolbox and lamp.

The miner's life was made up of waking up before dawn to sometimes walk a mile or more underground to get where he needed to begin his job only to be paid around one dollar a day, depending on how much coal he brought in. Since a miner was paid by a load of coal in a car, not the number of hours he worked, any job that did not directly produce coal was considered "dead work" for which the miner wasn't compensated. Dead work included drilling holes, preparing for a blast, breaking through walls with a pick and axe, clearing away debris from a blast or the tracks that moved the coal cars and even washing down the coal before it traveled to the breaker to get impurities like rock and slate removed. These jobs could take hours to do and could be extremely difficult, but a miner never got a cent for that time.

Even though a miner was basically treated as if he were an independent contractor, where the difficulties of removing the coal were his concern and not the mine owner's, the miner lost his freedom with the coal when it came time to sell it. Once the coal left the mine, it was the property of the mine owner, and he controlled how much he would pay a worker based solely on his own estimation of the amount of coal a car contained. Some miners even ended up with less than a dollar a day depending on how the mine owner priced the load that the worker brought in.

To add insult to injury, coal companies and their operators were not known for their willingness to take care of the many problems that plagued their workers as they were getting the coal product that they needed. In the famous song "Sixteen Tons," the line "I sold my soul to the company store" stands out because of the truth behind it. In the book *Struggle and Lose, Struggle and Win* by Elizabeth Levy and Tad Richards, the authors explain just how much a coal company owned and what this meant for a miner: "Most of the coal mines were in unpopulated regions and workers had to be brought to them. Housing was built for the miners by the operators on company-owned land. The company owned all the houses, the health facilities, the stores, even the churches. The company controlled all rents, and all prices at the store. Through these means, the company could make sure that the workers were always in debt to the company." The miner was stuck in a web of constantly trying to pay back his debt while also trying to take care of his family. The company he worked for always made sure that his rent and food were higher than he could afford just so he would have to borrow money from his next week's pay, and the company usually got back all of the money it paid out at the company store, where prices for tools and things that a miner's family needed were sky high. A miner was literally stuck in a vicious cycle, where he couldn't try to ask for better working conditions because of the debt he was in.

As stated before, all of this work for whatever little money they got was done in near pitch darkness with only a headlamp to find their way. Unlike today's LED headlamps attached to hard hats that can afford a fairly good field of vision, miners at the turn of the century could see only what a small lamp flame could allow, which was only what was in front of their faces and not much else. The oil wick lamps used were shaped like small tea kettles and were attached to lamp brackets on the forehead of a cloth cap with a leather brim. These were bare wicks that gave off a lot of smoke and were even known to ignite flammable gases in the mine, and the cap gave little protection to the head if there were cave-ins.

THE UNAVOIDABLE DANGERS

The threat of igniting flammable gases and being caught under a cave-in were just a few of the everyday dangers that coal workers went through. One of the biggest and most infamous accidents involved in the mines were explosions caused by gases trapped within the mine. The gas given off the most by coal is what is known as "fire damp" or "marsh gas." This gas is made of four parts hydrogen to one part carbon and is the product of vegetable decomposition during the formation of coal. Since this gas is half the weight of air, it rises to the roof of the mine and is in an explosive state when mixed with four to twelve times its volume of atmospheric air. Whenever a miner's exposed lamp wick came into contact with a large portion of this gas, an explosion was possible.

Gases in the mine not only caused explosions but were also harmful to breathe in. "Black damp," which is a carbonic acid gas that contains two parts oxygen to one part carbon, is heavier than air, so it sinks to the floor of a mine. A small amount of this gas can be breathed in without immediate danger besides dullness and numbness of the body, but if it is continually breathed in, unconsciousness and death can follow. This gas was mostly found in abandoned workings where a large concentration would accumulate over time.

One of the most dangerous gases found in the mines is called "white damp," or carbon monoxide, and is made up of equal parts oxygen and

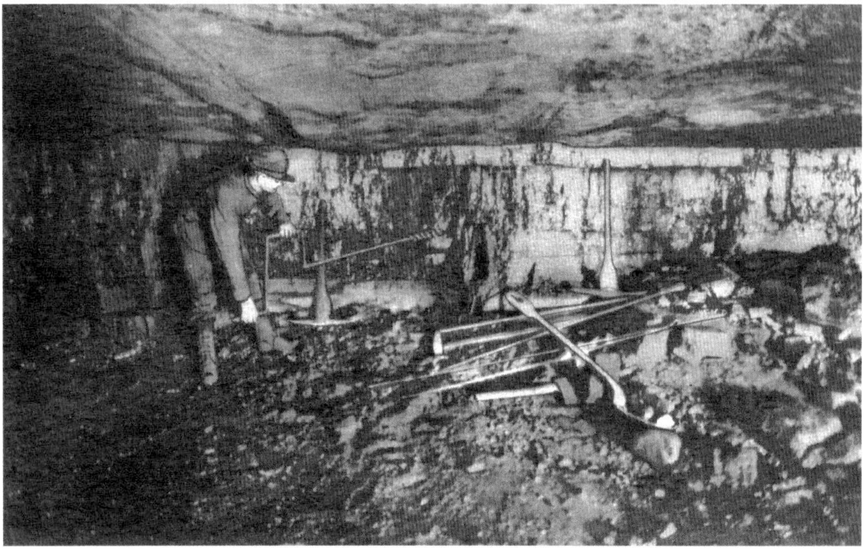

Drilling a hole in a vein of anthracite coal.

carbon. This particular gas is tasteless and odorless, and its presence cannot be detected before damage is done. To inhale a small portion of the gas could cause death. The gas was produced by any type of fire in the mines—including shaft fires, burning timbers and smoldering gob fires—and would cause more fatalities after an explosion occurred. One of the most dreaded gases of all time, it and an accumulation of black damp were the main causes of death in the Avondale mine disaster of 1869, in which two hundred miners, laborers and mule boys perished because of the gases given off by a fire that started in a ventilating furnace. Because safety precautions were so lax at the time, there was only one way to escape the mine, and not all of the workers made it out before asphyxiating.

Later on, as technology found its way deep into the veins, there were more ways to test for gases like carbon monoxide, and preventive measures were put in place to make sure an accidental explosion could not happen; however, in the late nineteenth century, all miners had were canaries and oil wick lamps. Canaries (and sometimes mice) were used to test an area of a mine to see if any poisonous gases were present. After a mine fire or an explosion, rescuers would go into the vein with a canary in a small wooden or metal cage. If the canary showed any signs of distress, such as swaying and falling off its perch, the miners would know that carbon monoxide was present and that it was too dangerous to work.

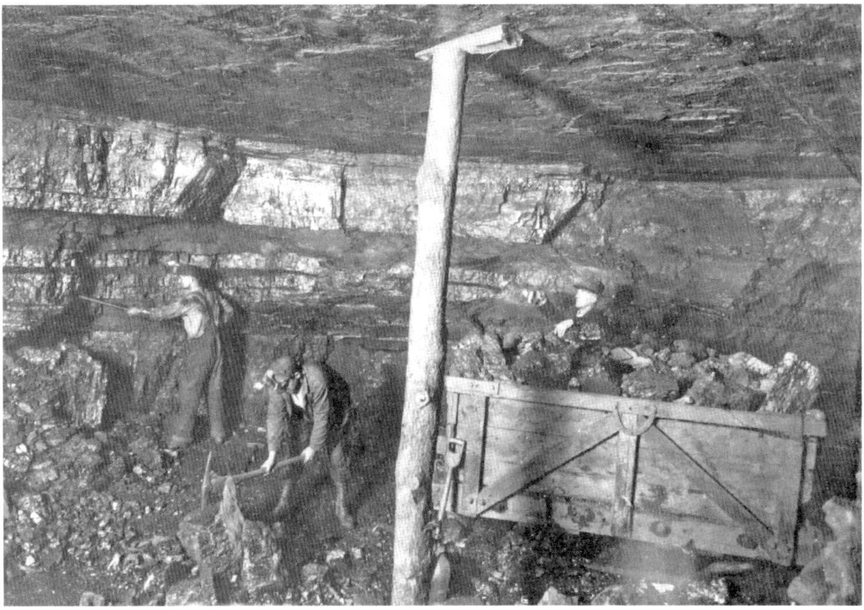

These miners work far away from the sunlight in a room with the floor, walls and ceiling made of coal.

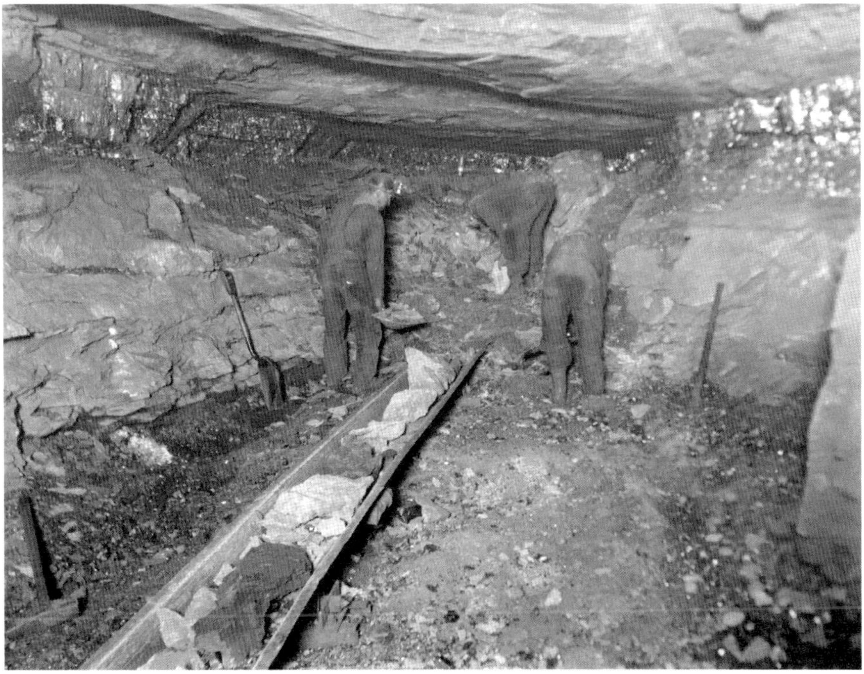

Miners loading rock in a chute.

The safety lamp was an even more effective way to find out what type of gas could be trapped within the mine. Unlike the flame attached to the miner's cap, the flame in this lamp was protected by a fine mesh. If the gas detected turned out to be fire damp, the flame would burn brighter because the flame attracts the gaseous air. If it was black damp, the flame went out due to the lack of oxygen caused by the gas.

These precautions didn't always help, and the dangers of the mine were as unpredictable as they were awful. Noxious and flammable gases, cave-ins, fires and flooding were fairly common. Long-term effects of working in a mine were just as life threatening. Prolonged inhalation of coal dust resulted in what is known as coal workers' pneumoconiosis, commonly called black lung disease or miner's asthma. Immediate aches and pains from being constantly stooped or crawling along a vein too small to stand up in easily turned into crippling arthritis in miners' later years.

THE BOYS OF THE MINES

These dangers didn't start when these men became miners either. Boys as young as twelve—or even younger if they lied about their age—worked in and around the mines, and there was no shortage of accidents. A nipper, also known as a "trapper," "trap boy" or "door boy," opened and closed the doors to mine shafts for ventilation and also to let the mule-driven wagons through the door when they left with a load of coal. The nipper, who was usually under fourteen years old, could spend hours just sitting in the dark waiting to open and close the door, and if he didn't pay attention or dozed off while waiting, he could be crushed by the door he was supposed to watch or even run over by a wagon trying to go back into the mine.

A mule boy, or driver, was, as his name implies, in charge of the care and transportation of the mules that pulled the coal wagons through the mines. These boys, who would hitch a mule to about four to seven empty cars at a time and guide them through the mine, faced the same types of dangers as a laborer or a miner, but they were also in danger if their mule got scared and became violent in the tight space of a mine or if they got caught under the wheels of the coal wagons.

The job that most miners, mule boys and nippers started out with was the infamously known breaker boy position. A breaker boy, who was usually twelve or under, worked outside the mines in a breaker where sharp, fast-

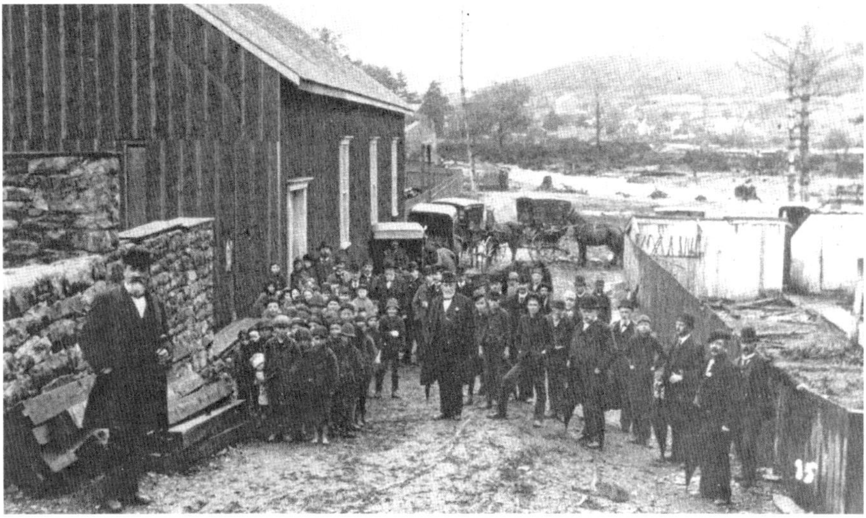

Breaker boys anxiously waiting for their earnings on payday.

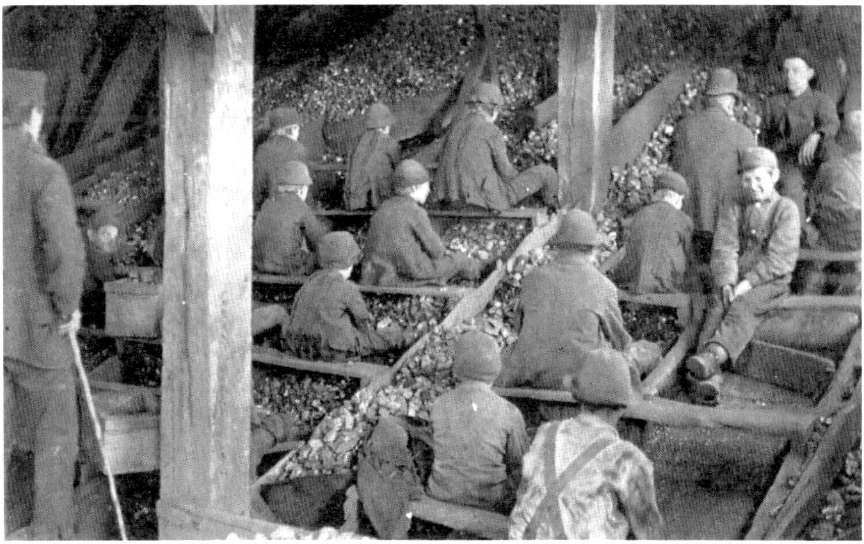

Breaker boys at work.

moving coal was sent through chutes for the boys to pick out the impurities of rock and slate before the coal was shipped to wherever it was needed. This boy worker would wake up at five thirty in the morning and by seven o'clock would be sitting on a hard bench built across the chute, picking out stone

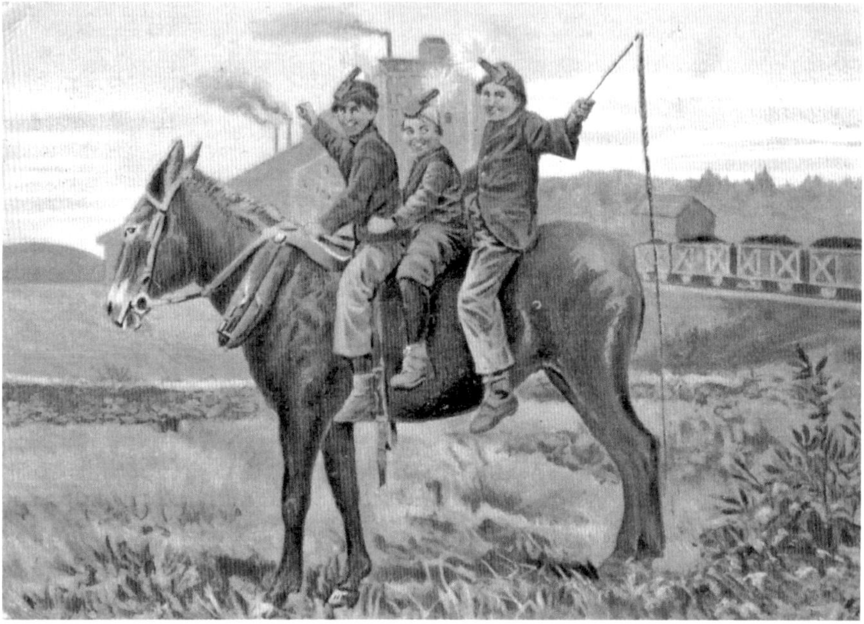

Boys as young as twelve and some even younger worked various jobs in the mines.

and slate as it flew in a steady stream through his fingers. When first starting out, a breaker boy's fingertips would be constantly cracked and bleeding from the sharp coal. It would take weeks for his hands to harden from the work. Not only was the inhalation of coal dust an ever-present problem, but the boy's boss was usually a stickler for productivity and wielded a wooden cane to use on any boy who slacked just a little. If he fell asleep, he wasn't only in danger of a sharp whack with a cane but also of actually falling into the chute and getting buried under piles of coal. The life of a working boy was as tough and dangerous as the work of a miner, and as Reverend McDowell so succinctly put it, "But however favorable the conditions, the boy's life is a hard one. Yet it is a consistent introduction to what is to follow."

OUTSIDE OF THE ACCIDENTS

Obviously an accident or disaster in the mine was awful for anyone involved, and that could even include rescue efforts by other miners. Rescue missions were a perilous task that could end in the life of another miner who was just trying

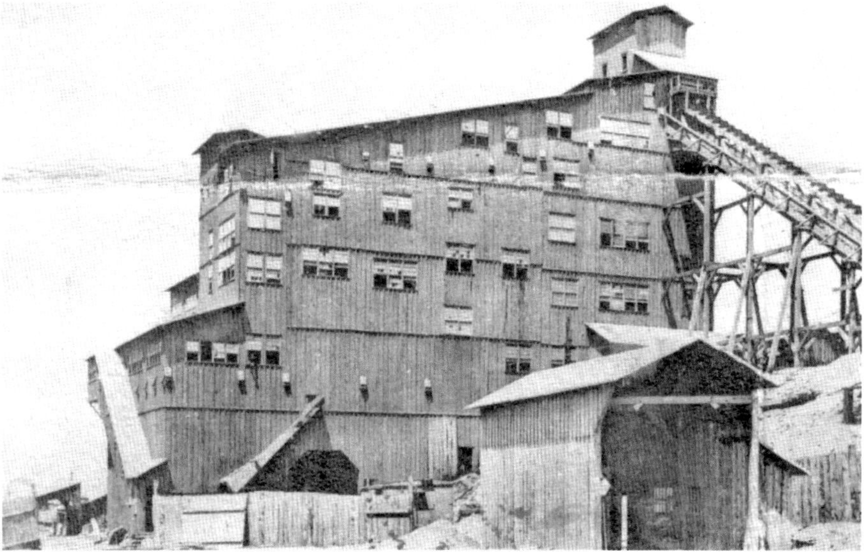

A view of the Green Ridge Colliery and Breaker.

to save his fellow man. These rescue efforts, besides being dangerous, could go on for days depending on the situation of the accident or disaster. As rescuers searched for survivors, authorities would try to figure out what exactly was going on in the mine while rumors would spread through the surrounding shantytown as to what caused the disaster, who survived and who was injured.

The most affected by the events of an accident was any relative of a miner, who had to anxiously wait for news about their loved one. The first sign of a disaster was the colliery whistle, which would sound a twenty-second blast when a disaster occurred. Family members would immediately flood the entrance to the colliery or mine, waiting for hours on end just to hear what happened to whom.

Besides anxiety, anger was always a prevalent emotion among the waiting crowd. It was usually aimed at the company authorities, who, instead of trying to calm the fears of waiting families, were known for covering up information or not releasing enough of it.

When the bodies of the victims were finally taken from the mine and brought to the surface, they were sometimes placed in a wagon called the Black Maria, which was pulled by two horses. This wagon served the purposes of either transporting an injured miner to his home or to a hospital or transporting a dead miner to his home so his wife or a relative could prepare his body for the wake and funeral to follow.

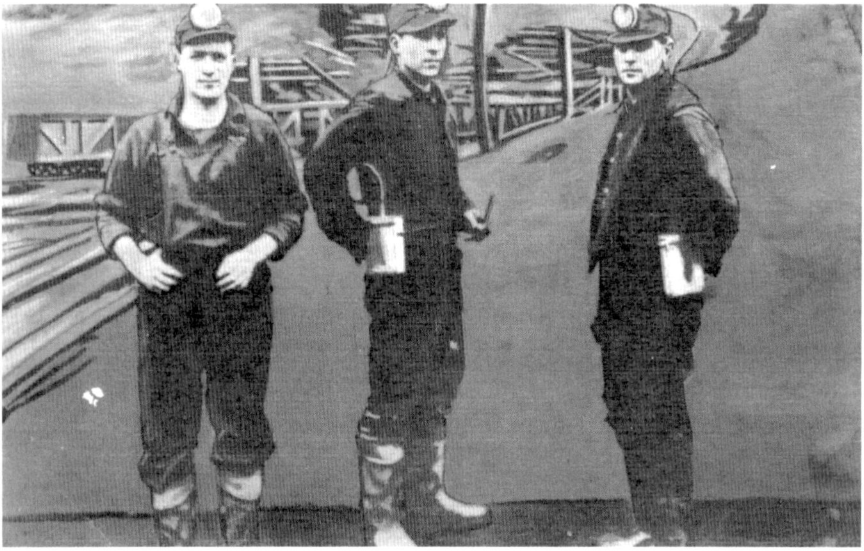

According to the Lackawanna County Coal Mine Guide, thirty-five thousand men and boys died in the anthracite mines of Pennsylvania from 1860 to 1966.

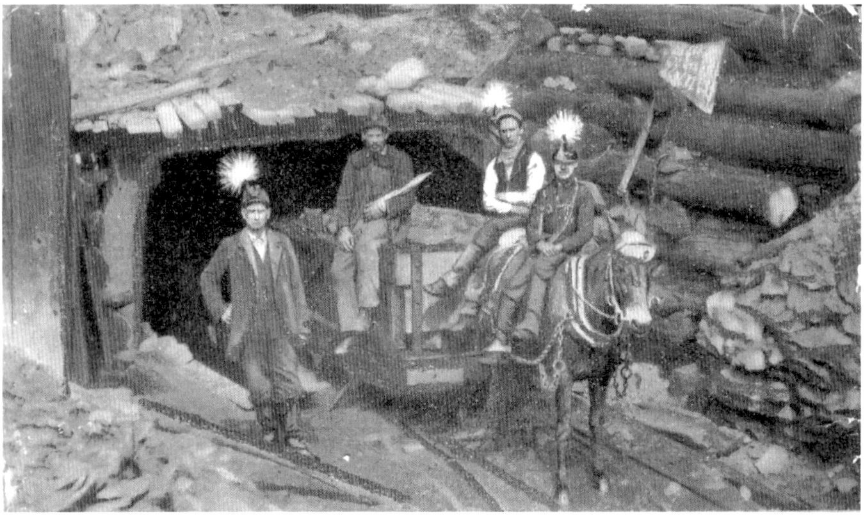

Tunnel entrance of coal mine.

By 1910, a few laws had been created to ensure safer working conditions for the miners (although not every colliery in Pennsylvania complied with these laws), and more resources were available to teach miners how to deal with slight to serious injuries in the mines thanks to a Scranton doctor named Matthew Shields and the help of the American Red Cross. Pamphlets translated into different languages for the many nationalities of the workers and lessons given by trained instructors helped to make a miner more self-sufficient during a disaster or an everyday injury, especially when the company was unwilling to help or couldn't send help in time.

THE WIFE OF A MINER

In any case where a family member was lost in a mining disaster, the resulting grief of the family was devastating, but when it came to the loss of a miner who had a wife and children, the results could be worse. It was not uncommon for an immigrant woman with possibly more than one child to care for to lose her husband in the mines and be left with few options. Not to mention the fact that the company would want the house back for another miner and his family in an incredibly short time if she didn't pay back the debts she and her husband had accrued through rent and the company store. To pay back this debt, her options were limited to marrying another

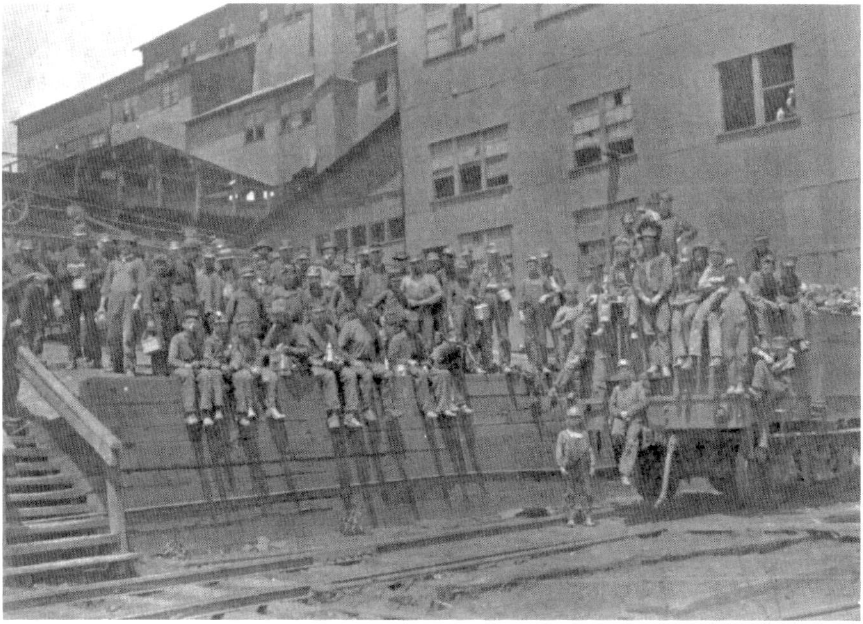

Breaker boys gathered together at dinner hour.

coal miner quickly or taking in boarders of single coal miners who would contribute some of their pay as rent.

In general, the coal miner's wife led a very strenuous and tiring life. Besides the ever-present anxiety of whether her husband would make it home alive from work, she ran her household completely on her own. Her job, which included keeping the house clean and her family fed, did not end when her husband came home after dark but could extend as late as midnight or beyond as she tried to keep order and peace.

With broom, dustpan and mop in hand, the miner's wife fought to keep the ever-present coal dust out of her home, hiding her hair in a dust cap as she went about her chores of keeping her shanty home as spotless as possible. Along with her daily cleanings, special cleanings for spring, fall and Christmas required a greater effort, including removing windows from their sashes to wash them, taking rugs out to be beaten and cleaning the floor with used, dampened tea leaves (these were later swept up, leaving a clean and shining floor behind).

With the bare minimum wage that a miner received, a wife did not have much to work with when it came to decoration, and what she bought in furniture usually came from the company store. The pieces were usually made from oak and sometimes had black leather upholstery, and for the bedroom, she was able to get iron bedsteads with cotton mattresses.

The household usually had at least one rug, and that belonged in the living room. The rug was made from coarse muslin that was used in the mine to block off dangerous or unused areas underground. These rugs were typically hand braided by the wife and took a lot of time to complete.

Curtains were sewed by the wife as well. The curtains were again made by the mine muslin that she could purchase at the company store, and some wives dyed them with coffee grounds, giving them a dark beige color called "ecrue." Sheets, pillow slips and towels were also made from the mine muslin. Potted plants, pictures and religious icons made up the rest of the decoration in a miner's home, all overseen and executed by his hardworking wife.

Along with the sewing and dyeing needed for household items, she would also make underwear for her entire family out of flour and potato sacks and would knit socks, stockings, caps and scarves for all of her children, which at that time would probably have been a large number.

With the making of most of her family's clothes, a miner's wife was also responsible for their cleaning and tried especially hard to clean out the ever-irritating coal dust. She would start bright and early on washday, going to the pump house to get the needed water that she would put into huge copper boilers on her stove. She would then boil and clean her family's laundry with homemade soap on a washing board until they were sparkling. A miner's clothes would never get fully clean, though, no matter how much lye she applied to the darkest areas.

Along with the clothing, she would wash her husband every day as well. When the miner returned from work, she would have her husband bathe in the kitchen in a zinc tub that she filled with hot water. The miner would then strip to his waist so she could scrub the dirt and dust off his back. When this was done, she would leave her husband alone to wash the rest of his body.

Cooking and baking were important tasks for the miner's wife as well. She would try to grow a plentiful garden during the summer and can a variety of food for the winter months. On one day a week, she would bake loaves of bread in a beehive oven in her backyard. She knew how to adapt to the rise and fall of prices at the company store and her husband's salary. In money matters, she tried her best to keep a good purse and was even known to go after her husband if he tried to squander a week's salary at a local bar.

The coal worker's wife did all of these things and more to the best of her ability at a time when nothing more was expected of her than to be dutiful and hardworking for her family and husband.

LIVING IN AMERICA

Society at large could also be a challenge for the largely immigrant population of the miners. The burgeoning middle class and the booming upper class were less than respectful to the people who worked to make their everyday life as comfortable as possible. While there were many individuals who were not rude or cruel or discriminatory to the people who flooded their country looking for work and opportunity, society as a whole seemed to turn down its nose at anyone who wasn't a natural-born citizen.

In an 1877 *Harper's New Monthly Magazine* article titled "The Miners of Scranton," Phoebe Gibbons breaks down the almost entirely immigrant population that worked in the Scranton mines. While she does give a detailed and well-executed insight into the working and social lives of the Welsh, Irish and a minority of Pennsylvania German coal workers, the tone throughout the article seems to fall into a constant battle of talking up the

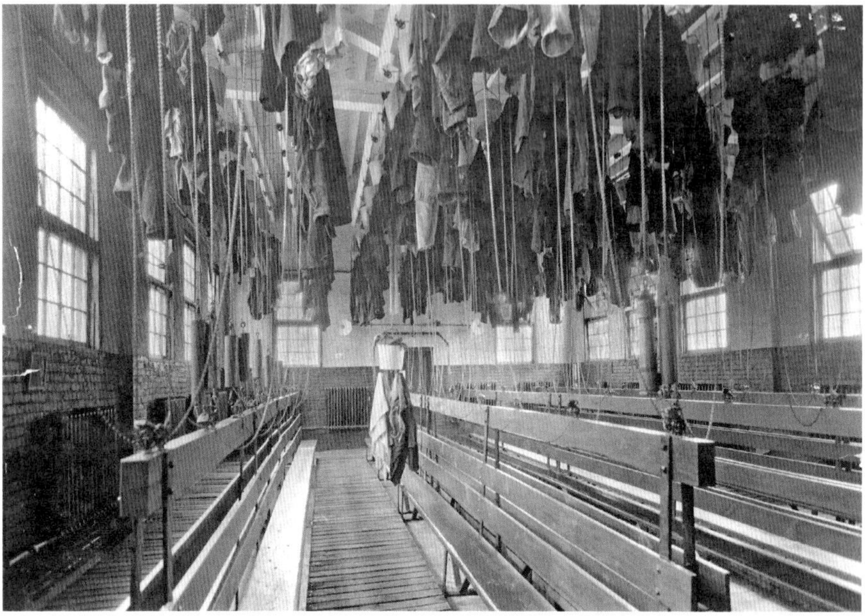

This area was used as a miners' changing room.

Welsh while simultaneously talking down the Irish, with the Germans as the happy medium. The sweeping generalizations peppered throughout this article give us an important look into this time period.

Gibbons describes the Welsh as "republicans almost to a man, and equally protestant; lovers of liberty, stubborn and enduring, not fickle," while she goes on to describe the Irish as "more volatile" and notes that "they do not practice much domestic economy; their motto is more 'come day, go day.' On a long strike they have generally nothing laid by for the emergency." She even interviewed a Catholic priest who said, "The Irish are not fit for bossing; they are kept in too much subjugation at home." The author beforehand ensures the reader that the Welsh are more "fit for bossing" because "they claim that they were never subjugated." This almost black-and-white comparison goes on for a while with the Welsh described as stoic and demure while the Irish were loud, enjoyed a good party and were usually publicly intoxicated.

This type of comparison and categorizing of immigrants went on through the decades as foreigners from different countries tried to find their way in the American landscape. In the 1870s and 1880s, one of the last wave of immigrants to come to America were the Italians, who were considered the lowest of the low, being described as "slovenly" and "unclean" compared to the Welsh and the Irish.

Immigrants were known to stick together, keeping up traditions from their homelands and a social life that included both foreign and American values that they gained from experience over time. For example, the Welsh celebrated St. David's day on the first day of March, even if it wasn't as big of a celebration in America; the Irish refused to work on St. Patrick's Day and enjoyed celebrating the Fourth of July because of their hatred of the English. It is also noted that these multicultural miners did interact with one another despite the fact that they were usually separated by their ethnicity in the mining towns. In the Gibbons article, a German miner said that between working lulls when a car loaded with coal was leaving the mine, the workers would rest for a moment, telling stories and cracking jokes with one another.

Though their lives were a constant struggle and the society they came to was not as forgiving as they hoped, the coal miners of Pennsylvania were a strong and diverse group of people who, through tragedy and struggles against their bosses and society at large, built America into a country of opportunity for generations to come.

3

VOICES OF LABOR AND CAPITAL

ROBERT H. MCKUNE

Scranton's fourth mayor was born in Newburg, New York, in August 1823. Today, McKune would be considered a renaissance man. His business career began at the age of thirteen as a shoe clerk. He later took over as proprietor of his mother's bakery before opening a grocery store in his hometown. The gold strike of 1849 lured the young McKune to the West Coast, where he became the first American to open a bakery in Panama.

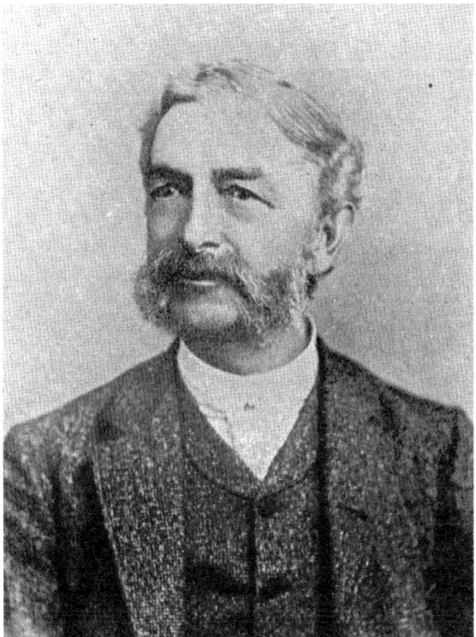

Scranton's fourth mayor, Robert H. McKune, sustained a broken jaw during his term in office.

At the age of thirty-nine, McKune came to reside in Scranton. It was 1862, and the Civil War was raging on. McKune became a first lieutenant in the Keystone Guards, who joined the Army of the Potomac and fought at Antietam. At the end of the war, McKune stayed in the South for a time before returning to Scranton, where he opened an insurance business. In 1868, he was appointed a U.S. commissioner, and in 1875, he was nominated by the Democratic Party to run for mayor of Scranton, a race in which he was victorious.

In 1877, Mayor McKune found himself in the middle of a major labor conflict between the workers and the owners of the railroads and coal mines. During the August 1, 1877 riot on Lackawanna Avenue, the mayor confronted the mob and asked them to peacefully cease and desist. The mob turned against the mayor, and his efforts resulted in a broken jaw, from which he recovered. He served out the rest of his term as mayor and was defeated by Terrence V. Powderly in 1878.

While on a visit with his sister in Newburg, New York, McKune suffered a fatal attack on October 9, 1894.

The following is a part of Mayor McKune's eulogy given by Dr. Samuel C. Logan of the First Presbyterian Church: "He was one of the good men and true who stood ready to sacrifice anything to make the city a home of righteousness."

REVEREND SAMUEL CROTHERS LOGAN, DD, LLD

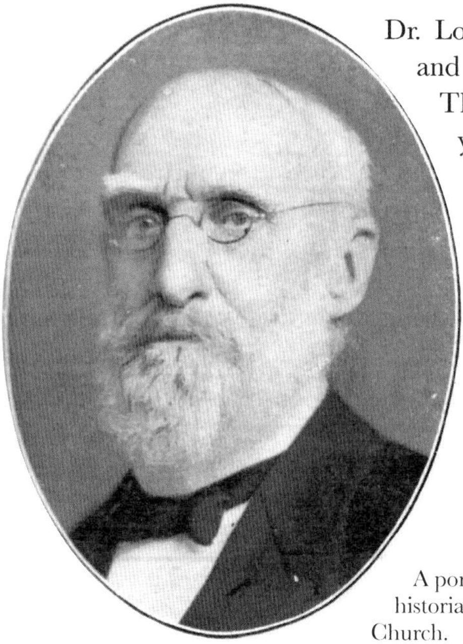

A portrait of Samuel Crothers Logan, local historian and reverend of the First Presbyterian Church.

Dr. Logan arrived in Scranton in 1868 and began his spiritual work here on Thanksgiving Day. The following year, he was installed as pastor of the First Presbyterian Church. During his time as pastor, he organized an Italian mission, and upon his retirement in 1892, the presbytery appointed him to organize a mission for the education of the thousands of coal miners in the Lackawanna and Wyoming Valleys. Despite his exceptionally busy schedule, Dr. Logan penned several books, including *A City's Danger and Defense*, a history of the 1877 riots in Scranton.

On August 23, 1877, he was made chaplain of the Scranton City Guard and later was given the same position when it became the Thirteenth Regiment. Because of his involvement during the riots, the Scranton City Guard also appointed him as the organization's historian. In Dr. Logan's own words, his book chronicling the riots "was a labor of love in order to preserve the history of the city."

TERENCE V. POWDERLY

Mr. Powderly was a native to the area, born in Carbondale, a city not far from Scranton, on January, 22 1849. He was a trained machinist and moved to Scranton to work at his craft on the Delaware, Lackawanna and Western Railroad when he was twenty. During his time in their employment, he attempted to organize workers for the Machinists' and Blacksmiths' International Union and was fired for the very same reason.

In 1876, he founded the Greenback-Labor Club in Scranton. The Greenback Labor Party sought to legalize unions' rights and called for the end of government corruption. Two years later, Powderly was elected mayor of Scranton, at a time when the people of the city felt it was in need of a change, and Powderly's conviction to labor and workingmen fit the bill, especially with the memories of the riot less than a year old. He was reelected as mayor in 1880 and again in 1882. While in office, he established a board of health, a sewage system, a new police force and a fire department.

In 1879, Powderly was nominated to head the Knights of Labor, succeeding Uriah Stephens as grandmaster workman. At the time, the Knights was the nation's largest labor organization; Powderly remained in the position until 1893. In the beginning, the Knights of Labor flourished under his leadership. The Knights reached its membership peak of 700,000 in 1885 after a victorious strike against Jay Gould's railroads. But that number would soon decline drastically as the organization was overshadowed by the American Federation of Labor.

The Knights of Labor was also frowned on by the Roman Catholic Church. The clergy suspected labor movements as being socialist. Their opposition took a personal turn for Powderly when on May 19, 1878, Reverend William O'Hara, the bishop of Scranton, denounced the labor organization and Powderly in particular. The Associated Press quoted the bishop as saying the following about Powderly:

> *I warned you against these secret societies; they are devised by designing men to dupe the unwary and draw them into their toils for the purpose of using them as tools for their own personal advancements. We have one instance of it in this city in a man who had hoodwinked the workingman into electing him mayor. He is a busybody and a slanderer. He has circulated the rumor that I have approved one of these secret societies; I have not even considered it. He is a fraud, an imposter, and I warn you against his scheming. Beware of being misled by such a character. Have nothing to do with him.*

According to Powderly's biography, he considered the reverend's harsh words an excommunication. The Roman Catholic Church did not change its dim view of the Knights of Labor until the archbishop of Baltimore, being more liberal, was able to lift the ban of the labor organization in 1887.

Terence Powderly declined a fourth run for Scranton's mayor in hopes of a congressional nomination from the Democratic Party, but his hopes were soon dashed when no nomination came. His disappointment led him to campaign for the position of head of a new federal government agency, the Bureau of Labor Statistics. Powderly was again passed over for this post because his critics felt his thinking was too radical for the times.

Powderly did not stray far from the city. As the grandmaster of the Knights of Labor, he preferred to work out of his West Scranton home rather than the national headquarters located in Philadelphia. But that would change in 1896 with the election of President William McKinley. Powderly was appointed commissioner general of immigration and moved to Washington, D.C., where he lived until his death in 1924.

WILLIAM WALKER SCRANTON

The family for whom Scranton is named put the city on the industrial map with the birth of its iron furnaces in 1840. William Walker was the eldest son of Joseph Hand Scranton. He resided in the city from birth and attended Yale University during the time of the Civil War. After graduation, W.W. returned to Scranton to begin his career in the family business. He apprenticed for two years at the works of the Lackawanna Iron and Coal Company, of which his father was president. In 1871, he was appointed assistant to the president and later superintendent of all the company mills. During the early 1870s, he traveled abroad in order to follow the study of Bessemer steel manufacture as practiced in French and German plants. Upon his return home, he was made general manager of the Lackawanna Iron and Coal Company and, at once, put his newly acquired knowledge into action by constructing a Bessemer steel rail mill and works, thereby doubling the capacity of manufacturing and improving the quality.

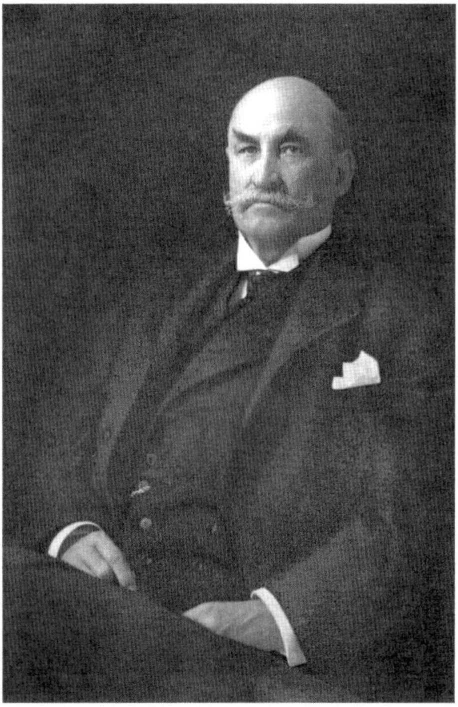

William Walker Scranton, president of the Lackawanna Iron and Coal Company.

During the Great Railroad Strike of 1877, the workers of the Lackawanna Iron and Coal Company were the first to walk out in protest of the continuing wage decreases. W.W. was deep in labor troubles. On August 1, 1877, he and twenty-five of his men met the members of the Scranton Citizens' Corps at the intersection of Lackawanna and Washington Avenues and faced the three to five thousand rioters. Mr. Scranton, along with others, was arrested and put on trial for manslaughter, but they were all acquitted by the court.

In 1880, due to a disagreement, Scranton resigned his position at the ironworks and embarked in the steel business independently, organizing the Scranton Steel Company. In 1891, the Lackawanna Iron and Coal Company and Scranton Steel merged.

COLONEL HENRY MARTYN BOIES

In 1865, Henry Martyn Boies came to the city as a member of the powder firm of Laflin, Boies, and Tarck, of Saugerties, New York. The firm purchased a plant in Archbald and erected another in Moosic. The business was a success, and Boies was made president and general manager of the Moosic Powder Company.

During the riots of 1877, Boies and his family were out of town, but upon hearing of the tragic events, he quickly returned home in time to take part in the formation of the Scranton City Guard, of which he was made commanding officer with the rank of major.

When the guard was turned into the the Thirteenth Regiment National Guard of Pennsylvania, Colonel Boies was made commandant for five years, from 1878 to 1883, during which time he obtained the title of colonel.

EZRA H. RIPPLE

Scranton's seventh mayor (1886–90) was born on February 14, 1842, in Mauch Chunk, Pennsylvania. Today, it is known as Jim Thorpe. Four years later, his family moved to Scranton, where they eventually settled in the Hyde Park area. During the Civil War, Ripple enlisted in the regular army under the command of Colonel H.M. Holt of K Company Fifty-third Pennsylvania Infantry. During an attack on Fort Johnson in Charleston Harbor on July 3, 1864, Ripple, along with 140 other soldiers, was captured by the Confederates and taken to the infamous Andersonville Prison. Conditions at the prison have been compared to twenty-five acres of hell on earth. By the end of the war, it was estimated that 14,000 inmates died of disease and starvation. Ripple remained a prisoner at Andersonville for two and a half months before being transferred to another prison in South Carolina for an additional eight months. Ripple and several of the other prisoners found a way to escape from this minimum-security prison only to be recaptured. A month later, he was released, and on June 30, 1865, he was granted an honorable discharge from the army.

During the labor unrest of 1877 in the city, Ripple joined forces with other Civil War veterans to form an organization of special citizens in order to help Mayor McKune maintain order. Ripple was named captain of this organization, called the Scranton Citizens' Corps and later the Scranton City Guard. In 1878, it was incorporated with the Thirteenth Regiment of the Pennsylvania National Guard, and Captain Ripple was promoted to major. He was made colonel in 1888 and served until 1896.

In July 1892, Colonel Ripple led the Thirteenth Regiment when it was called on to perform riot duty at Homestead, Pennsylvania, just outside Pittsburgh. Steel workers employed by Carnegie Steel clashed with union-busting Pinkerton detectives and private police employed by the company. Riot duty lasted for two weeks before the regiment was able to return to the city.

Ripple was later appointed postmaster of Scranton in 1897 and reappointed in 1901 by President Theodore Roosevelt and then again in 1909 by President Taft. Colonel Ezra Ripple passed away on November 19, 1909.

FREDERICK LYMAN HITCHCOCK

Colonel F.L. Hitchcock wore many hats during his lifetime—lawyer, soldier, author, just to name a few. On August 22, 1862, he entered the army as adjutant of the 132nd Regiment Pennsylvania Volunteers. He participated in some of the bloodiest conflicts of the Civil War, including Antietam, Chancellorsville and Fredericksburg, where he was badly wounded and left for dead on the battlefield. In December 1863, he was appointed lieutenant colonel of colored troops and organized the 25th Regiment United States Colored Troops of Philadelphia.

His time in the war prepared him for the labor strife the city would face more than a decade later. Like many of the Civil War veterans in Scranton, Hitchcock answered the mayor's call for volunteers of the Scranton Citizens' Corps. His military knowledge and

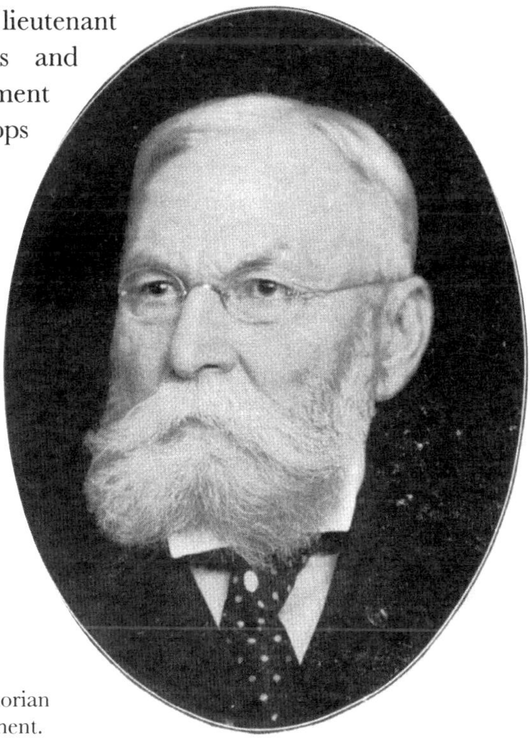

Frederick L. Hitchcock, author, historian and officer of the Thirteenth Regiment.

experience were again called on to assist in the organization of the Scranton City Guard. Colonel Hitchcock refused to take an office, but upon request of his good friend H.M. Boies, he accepted the appointment of adjutant. In 1878, upon the formation of the Thirteenth Regiment, National Guard of Pennsylvania, Hitchcock did accept the position of lieutenant colonelcy. According to Hitchcock, the events of 1877 proved the necessity of a first-class regiment to which he freely gave his time and experience to perfect. After Colonel H.M. Boies declined reelection in 1883, Hitchcock took over as leader of the Thirteenth Regiment and eagerly served until 1888.

During his second year as colonel, he succeeded in qualifying all the men in the regiment as marksmen in rifle practice. They were the first regiment to reach that standard in the history of the National Guard at that time. Despite all the good work he did for the regiment, he declined a second term and was presented by his fellow officers with a plaque, which was inscribed with the following: "He led the regiment from the left to the right of the line, and stood with it at the head of the National Guard of Pennsylvania."

CLARENCE DARROW

Clarence Darrow's first job was that of a farmhand, but he found it to be too difficult and turned his focus to studying law. He passed the bar in 1877, labeled the bloodiest year for labor violence; it was perhaps a premonition of what was yet to come. Darrow was often identified with labor by appearing as counsel for the coal miners during several disputes. In 1887, he took part in attempts to free the anarchists charged with murder in the Haymarket Riot in Chicago. Three years later, he became general attorney for the Chicago and North Western Railway Union. He left the position in order to defend Eugene V. Debs, president of the American Railway Union arrested on a federal charge of contempt in court arising from the Pullman Strike of 1894. Even though Debs was convicted, Darrow established a national reputation as a labor and criminal lawyer.

In Scranton, he represented the workingmen during the 1902 Coal Strike Commission Hearings that began in November at the Lackawanna County Courthouse.

He was often called "a fighter for lost causes"; ironically, he won most of those lost causes.

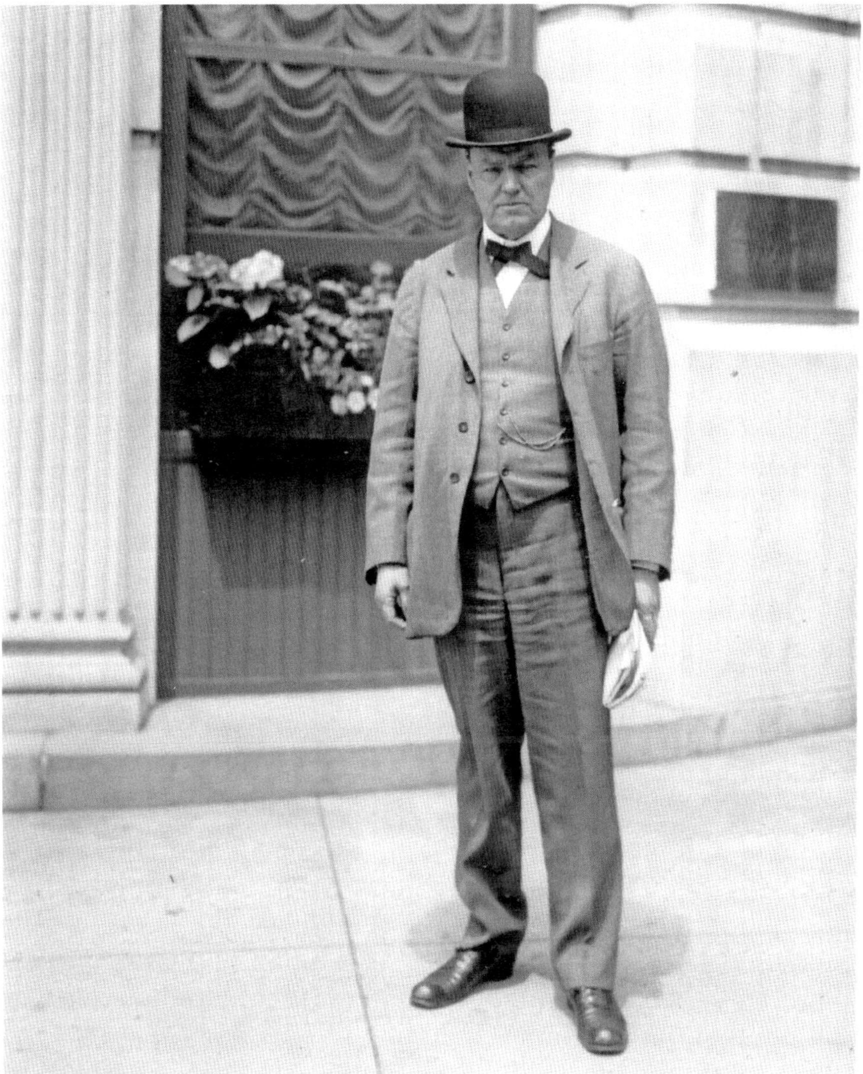

Famous lawyer Clarence Darrow defended the laboring class during the 1902 Anthracite Strike hearings. While in Scranton, Mr. Darrow took up occupancy at the Hotel Jermyn.

The following is a portion of Clarence Darrow's closing arguments on behalf of the United Mine Workers before the Anthracite Coal Commission on February 13, 1903:

> *If the work of this commission does not result in getting rid of this abominably, disgraceful evil of child labor in Pennsylvania, then I think*

the people may well say that it has been a failure. You may not get rid of it at once, but no man ever lived that could make an excuse for it. I do not think any man ever lived that would not blush because of the money he gets from it. I was surprised that my friend Reynolds in his zeal should defend it, defend the taking of a boy 12 years old, and setting him down to labor in this everlasting cloud, for 10 hours, or any hours—for what? That you may get gold. That is all. Can any man frame an honest defense for it? Where are your sons and your daughters? Let me say this, that until you, Mr. Railroad President, or you Mr. Lawyer, will take your child by the hand and lead him up the breaker stairs and sit him down to pick at that trough of moving coal, until you will take your pale girl to the silk mills, let me speak for the children of the poor. Is there any one who can defend it? This custom has grown up in the State of Pennsylvania because there is money in it, and the industries of Pennsylvania are dependent upon it. Shame upon the industries of Pennsylvania if this is true! If it is so, of little avail have we protected this great State for half a century, if the result of all of it is that men shall grow rich from the labor of these small children.

MOTHER JONES

The story of coal is always the same. It is a dark story. For a second's more sunlight, men must fight like tigers. For the privilege of seeing the color of their children's eyes by the light of the sun, fathers must fight as beasts in the jungle. That life may have some decency, something of beauty—a picture, a new dress, a bit of cheap lace fluttering in the window—for this, men who work down in the mines must struggle and lose, struggle and win.

—Mother Jones

Mother Jones was born Mary Harris in Cork, Ireland, on approximately August 1, 1837. Since her family lived in almost abject poverty, her father, Richard Harris, moved to America in 1835 and sent for his family not long after. Even though Jones was brought up in Toronto, Canada, her family were still considered American citizens because her father worked as a laborer with a railway construction crew, and she was always proud of that distinction.

When she grew older, she became a teacher, and her first position was in a convent in Monroe, Michigan. When she grew tired of "bossing little children," she went to her other talent of dressmaking and opened up a shop

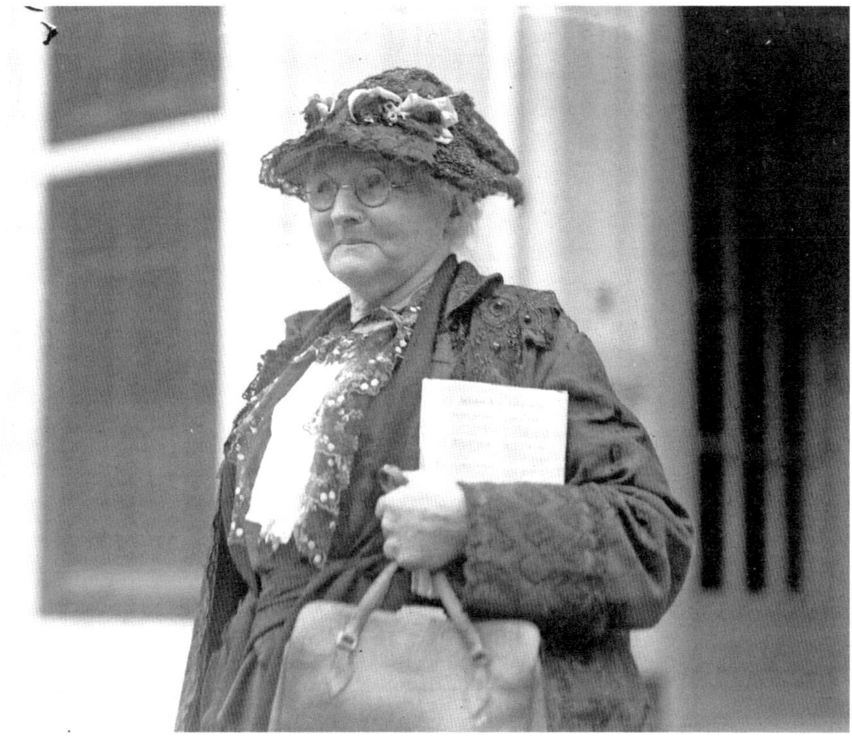

In 1903, labor leader and activist Mary Harris, better known as Mother Jones, led a protest march of mill children from Philadelphia to New York.

in Chicago. Shortly after, though, she would return to teaching, this time in Memphis, Tennessee. This is where she met and married her husband, George E. Jones, a "staunch member" of the Iron Moulders' Union, in 1861. In 1867, during a yellow fever epidemic in Memphis, Mary's four children, along with her husband, passed away, and she was left "alone through nights of grief" as other families of her neighborhood went through the same heartache. After the union buried her husband, she helped with the nursing of others who suffered from the fever and did so until the plague was over.

After that tragedy, she moved back to Chicago and once more went into the dressmaking business, her shop being located on Washington Street near a lake. During this time, she made dresses for the "aristocrats" of Chicago who lived on Lake Shore Drive, while watching the poor and homeless from her shop window, knowing that her "employers seemed neither to care or notice."

In October 1871, the Great Chicago Fire displaced thousands of people who lost their homes and businesses to the flames. Mother Jones was not spared. She lost her shop and everything she had, forcing her, her business partner and others to stay through the next day on the lakefront without food. She later took refuge at St. Mary's Church until she could find a new place to stay, and during that stay, she discovered that in a nearby building, meetings for the Knights of Labor were being held. She spent many evenings listening to speakers and even spent Sundays, when they held meetings in the woods, with the labor group.

She was impressed with the fight and fire of the union and considered that time of the labor movement as "the days of sacrifice for the cause of labor. Those were the days when we had no hall, when there were no high salaried officers, no feasting with the enemies. Those were the days of the martyrs and the saints." Shortly after, at the age of thirty-four, Mary became an active part of the Knights of Labor and became involved with her first strike.

From 1880 through the rest of her life, Mary Harris Jones treated the fight for labor as if it were her family. Styling herself as Mother Jones, she was known for her white hair, severe black clothing, confrontational attitude and willingness to do whatever it took for struggling laborers to get the rights that they deserved.

In the 1890s, Jones became an organizer for the United Mine Workers of America and was one of the first to travel to Pennsylvania to start organizing the anthracite mine fields. The first strike in Pennsylvania that she was involved in was a four-month-long strike that happened in Arnot. Eventually, this strike would become a victory on the side of the miners, but when Mother Jones arrived, spirits were low. When the operator of the mine found out that the union was getting involved, he retaliated by evicting striking families, including a family that was housing Jones. The company also started sending in nonunion "scab" workers to keep production going in the mines.

An enraged Mother Jones would not back down, and instead of letting the strikers go out to stop the scabs, Jones called on the miners' wives to strike out with mops, brooms and pots to cause a ruckus and to stop the scabs from working. She remarked in her autobiography that the leader of the women was an Irish woman wearing a red petticoat over her nightgown with one black and one white stocking and a little fringed shawl to cover her "wild red hair." She led the women to the entrance of the mine, and as the nonunion workers came up with the mules, the women started to yell and bang their pots and pans. When a sheriff told the leader of the group to stop making noise or she'd scare the mules, the woman replied by hitting the man with the tin wash pan she was holding and said, "To hell with you and the mules!"

These women whom Mother Jones helped to organize kept watch on the mine with "mops or brooms in one hand and babies in the other arm wrapped in little blankets" to make sure that no one would enter the mine. Soon after, coal production stopped altogether. The company was losing money daily, so it conceded to all of the miners' demands.

Mother Jones was also known for involvement in the Great Strike of 1902. She went from town to town during the strike to help make sure that the strikers were staying out of the mines and conferred with the UMWA's president at the time, John Mitchell. By the end of the six-month strike, Jones had become increasingly upset with how Mitchell was handling the fact that the coal operators refused to sit down with any of the labor leaders or even recognize the UMWA as a union. When the miners did not get everything that they demanded and what they did get was not what they originally asked for, Jones was livid. She believed that Mitchell was too blinded by his admiration for Theodore Roosevelt, who, in an unprecedented act, got involved with ending the strike. She also believed that Mitchell was enjoying the flattery that he received from the public, which, for once, was on the side of labor, and that he was not helping as much as he should. In her autobiography she even stated, "Mr. Mitchell died a rich man, distrusted by the working people whom he once served."

After the 1902 strike, Mother Jones would continue her fight for justice for the rest of her life, giving all her time helping miners, silk mill workers, streetcar workers, steel workers and many more. She would "raise hell," get arrested multiple times and even be charged with conspiracy to commit murder, but nothing hampered her fighting spirit.

In her autobiography, which was originally published in 1935, famed attorney Clarence Darrow wrote the introduction and described Mary "Mother" Jones as "a woman of action fired by a fine zeal." He goes on to describe her as such: "She defied calumny. She was not awed by guns or jails. She kept on her way regardless of friend and foes. She had but one love to which she was always true and that was her cause."

She fought for the laborers up until she passed away on November 30, 1930, at the age of ninety-three. She is buried at the Union Miners Cemetery in Illinois next to victims of the Illinois mine riot of 1898.

JOHN MITCHELL

John Mitchell was born on February 4, 1870; he was only seven years old during the Great Railroad Strike of 1877. He grew up in a coal mining village in Illinois, and he entered the mines at a very young age as a trapper boy. In the 1880s, he tried mining in Colorado and Wyoming but returned to his home state frustrated and penniless. That was when he decided coal miners could achieve a better life if they worked together and formed a union. He joined a local Knights of Labor organization, but due to that organization's numerous unsuccessful strikes, Mitchell joined up with the United Mine Workers of America (UMWA) the very year it was founded in 1890. The following year, he married Katherine O'Rourke, a coal miner's daughter, and began to raise a family while studying law and social and economic issues. He rose rapidly within the union, and in January 1899, he was elected president of the UMWA. In the fall of that same year, he went to eastern Pennsylvania in an attempt to organize its anthracite fields. He found atrocious working conditions, low wages, long hours and a higher rate of industrial accidents than in the bituminous coal fields. The coal operations were being run by seven coal-transporting railroads, which, in turn, were controlled by capitalists J.P. Morgan and Cornelius Vanderbilt. After giving his report of the deplorable conditions of the Pennsylvania mine fields to the UMWA, Mitchell returned in August 1900 and called for a convention to be held in Scranton of the three anthracite districts in order to make a plan of

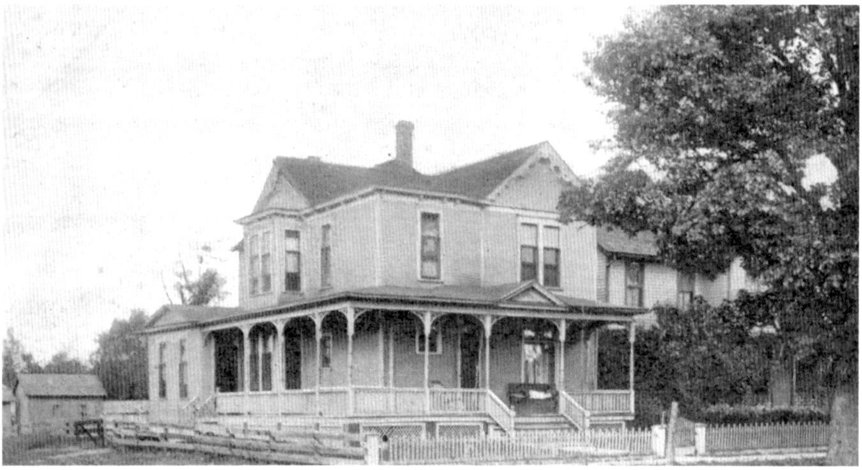

Pictured is the birth house of Johnny Mitchell. He was a native of Illinois and orphaned at the early age of six.

demands that would include a wage increase. The miners had not received a raise since 1880.

If the convention's demands were not met by the operators, the UMWA Executive Board gave Mitchell permission to call a strike. The operators ignored his request for arbitration, and the strike began on September 17, 1900; 112,000 workers responded to the work stoppage, and the strike was conducted with restraint.

By October 1, the Reading Company had posted a 10 percent wage increase, and on the twelfth of the month, a convention convened once again in Scranton in order to decide to accept that offer. It was accepted by the following day, provided that the agreement would not expire until April 1, 1901. The strike officially ended on October 29, 1900, the miners victorious. This date was later declared John Mitchell Day by the miners. Many historians consider the strike of 1900 a skirmish compared to the anthracite coal strike of 1902. Conditions in the mines had deteriorated to their lowest point, and the miners were willing to sacrifice what was needed to provide a better life for their families. The success for better wages and improved working conditions would depend on the United Mine Workers to organize the workers and convince the operators to accept their demands. John Mitchell, being the UMWA president, led the charge and planned out the strategy of the miners.

Their demands were as follows: an eight-hour workday, 20 percent increase in wages, a rate of sixty cents per ton fixed at 2,240 pounds and recognition by the operators of the union. The miners' demands were rejected by the operators. On May 13, an executive committee of miners ordered a work stoppage, and on May 15, despite Mitchell's opposition, the strike was extended. Mitchell urged the miners to work together and to keep it peaceful in order to avoid repeating the riots of 1877.

After many months, the strike ended on October 23, 1902. Mitchell saw it as a victory, but many of his critics did not, including his good friend Mother Jones, who fondly referred to him as comrade in their corresponding letters.

Mitchell served as the UMWA president until he resigned in 1908. In Mitchell's later years, he was a member of the New York State Workman's Compensation Commission in 1914, and in 1915, when the commission merged with the New York Department of Labor Industrial Commission, he was appointed chairman. He also served on the Federal Milk Commission, Federal Food Board for New York City, New York State Food Administration and the New York State Council of Farms and Markets.

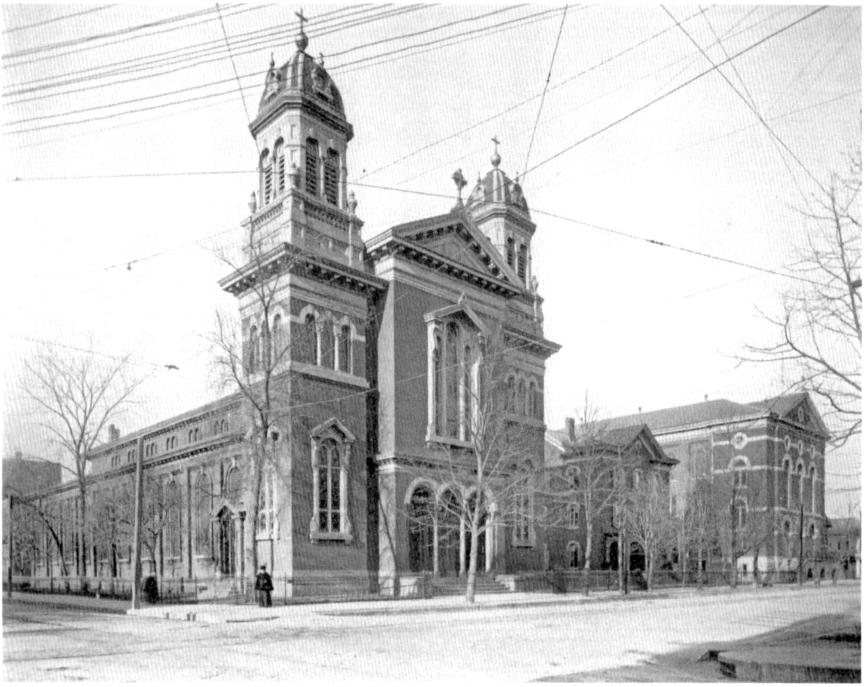

St. Peter's Cathedral on Wyoming Avenue in Scranton is where the funeral services of Johnny Mitchell took place. The labor leader is buried at the Cathedral Cemetery in West Scranton and chose this as his last resting place because he felt his biggest triumph occurred in Scranton.

In 1919, Mitchell passed away at the age of forty-nine from complications due to gallbladder surgery. But even after death, his connection to Scranton would remain. His funeral services were conducted at the Roman Catholic St. Peter's Cathedral of the Diocese of Scranton, and his body was interred at the Cathedral Cemetery in West Scranton.

4

The Great Strike That Affected a Nation

Our Country moved forward on the back of the workers and the unsung heroes of the Industrial Revolution.
—John Mitchell

Twentieth-Century America

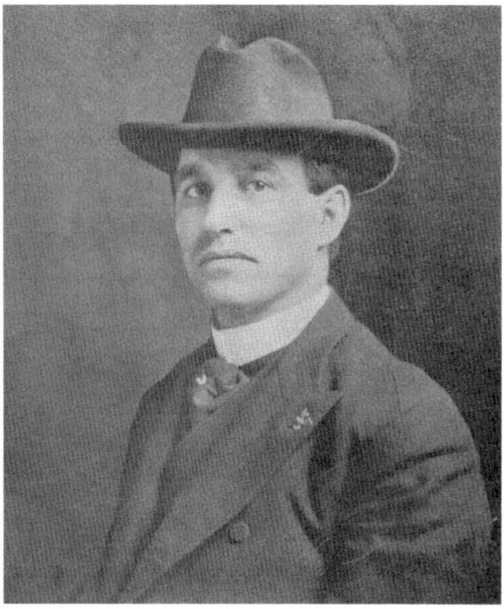

John Mitchell, labor leader and president of the United Mine Workers Association (1899–1908).

All through history, people have been known to fight for their rights. America itself was built on the idea that we had to fight for our certain inalienable rights of life, liberty and the pursuit of happiness. As the country progressed, grew larger and implemented advanced technology during the dawn of the twentieth century, that original idea of liberty and helping our fellow man seemed to lose its way. As capitalism grew with its many machines and its many cogs within it, society was in the classic situation where the ones with the money had the power to rule and ignored the people who had to work under them to survive.

By the late 1800s, this type of hierarchy ruled and reached every part of the country, including the anthracite coal fields of Pennsylvania, where men worked for unbearably long hours mining deep into the earth only to be paid in pennies or not be paid at all to do one of the most dangerous jobs in the world. By 1902, when the public and the government finally took notice of their strife, things had begun to change.

THE ERA OF THE BEAUTIFUL RICH

From about the 1890s to 1914, America was one of the most decadent places to be part of the upper class. Called *la Belle Époque*, or the "Beautiful Time," it was a period of time dedicated to luxuriating in the finer pleasures of life and living on the principle of *joie de vivre*. While this thought process was a part of everyday life in Paris, France, it was also exemplified in America and was at the forefront of society in the anthracite region of Pennsylvania, especially in Scranton.

Another definitive fact about this period of time was that it was the heyday of the "Edwardian era" that lasted from the death of the second-longest reigning monarch of England, Queen Victoria, in 1901 until four years after the death of King Edward VII, for whom the era was named, in 1914. This era defined a new European and American style that far transcended the reign of King Edward. The rich of this era got to experience the firsthand rewards of modern industrialization and mass-produced items and had a greater ability to indulge in fashion, entertainment, cuisine and travel as no other society had done before. The arts saw the introduction and popularity of Expressionism, Post-Impressionism, Cubism and the extremely popular Art Nouveau, which affected the designing of commercial art, architecture, household articles, jewelry and furniture and the emergence of curvaceous styles for women's clothing, symbolized by the ever-popular "Gibson Girl," such as the DL&W Railroad's Phoebe Snow.

This time in America was also affected by the growing tensions in Europe in what is known as the pre–World War I era (1871–1914). America had just started to join the mix of the European nations as they struggled with one another over rivalries, diplomatic realignments, colonial competitions and the rearmament of militaries. Those forty years of constant tension burst into the first "modern war," which became known for its unparalleled bloodshed.

As stated before, Scranton, Pennsylvania, reaped the benefits of the Edwardian era and the Beautiful Time for as long as they lasted. According to Robert A. Jansov in his essay "Beyond 'The Great Coal Strike': The Anthracite Region in 1902," as the coal industry expanded at the turn of the century and while there was an influx of eastern and southern Europeans coming to America to find work in urban areas, Scranton's population showed substantial growth:

> *By the 1870s, Scranton boasted an ethnically diverse population of 20,000 residents. By 1880, the city had over 45,000 people and was the largest city in northeastern Pennsylvania. The city's population more than doubled to 102,026 by 1900. If the populations of both the "urban fringe" and "outer fringe" communities either adjacent to or near Scranton are taken into consideration, the 1900 population of metropolitan Scranton was 186,320.*

Scranton was a booming city with a largely diverse business market. Even with the loss of Lackawanna Iron and Steel (Scranton's oldest and largest company) in 1901, when it moved the work to Buffalo, New York, "the assessed value of real estate in Scranton remained over sixty-five million dollars"—not to mention, $20 million of capital was invested in the more than seven hundred industries in the city. Jansov states:

> *Scranton's remaining industries, like the Dickson Manufacturing Company and the Scranton Stove Company that operated in the city since the 1850s, or the International Textbook Company, the Scranton Electric Construction Company, the Sauquoit Silk Manufacturing Company, the Scranton Button Manufacturing Company, the Scranton Lace Company, and the International Salt Company that emerged in the last decades of the nineteenth century, managed to employ over twelve thousand workers with combined payrolls over five million dollars. County-wide, another three hundred industries operated, making the total over one thousand manufacturing establishments operated by an equal number of proprietors. The total wages paid by these industries was over six million dollars, producing an average annual wage of four hundred dollars.*

In the city, there were more than seven hundred proprietors with more than six hundred salaried officials and clerks who earned an average of $1,198 annually. When combined with the industrial proprietors, these citizens made up an "affluent professional class" who lived in the more fashionable areas of Scranton like Madison Avenue, Clay Avenue, Washington Avenue, Green Ridge and the Hill Section.

Social clubs and societies were an enormous part of Scranton, and the city boasted more prestigious organizations than Wilkes-Barre with clubs that included the Scranton Country Club, the Scranton City Club, the Scranton Bicycle Club, the Scranton Engineering Club, the Physicians' Club and the Green Ridge Woman's Club—just to name a few.

Scranton enjoyed all that its bustling economy had to offer, and while the rich grew richer and more extravagant with each passing year, the poor of Scranton grew poorer. But they also started to fight for their right to a better life.

AND THE PROGRESSIVE POOR

Another cultural phenomenon that defined this period in time was the Progressive movement, which started in 1900 and lasted all the way through to 1917. What defined this era was almost the antithesis of the Edwardian and *la Belle Époque* periods of American history. This era was known for trying to find ways to use the American government for human welfare purposes. Reformers of the Progressive era fought against urban politics and robber barons and promoted child welfare, conservation, fair wages for fair labor and consumer protection, and they challenged the American idea of isolating itself from the rest of the world. They believed the country had "a moral obligation to spread democracy and economic opportunity to reap profits in foreign markets."

The Great Strike of 1902 and its outcome was considered a success that helped to propel the Progressive era through the rest of its years.

For the lower-class miners of Scranton and northeastern Pennsylvania, the Progressive thought of having a fair wage for fair labor was exactly what they were looking for, but the fight to get higher wages, safer working conditions and shorter days was an uphill battle against the uncompromising coal barons that started long before the 1902 strikes when groups like the Knights of Labor, the American Federation of Labor (AFL) and the Workers Benevolent Association (WBA) tried to unionize mine workers from the bituminous mine fields in Illinois to the anthracite fields of Pennsylvania.

While unions won some of these battles, many were lost, and in the worst cases, the unions were ignored. Their fight would then get buried

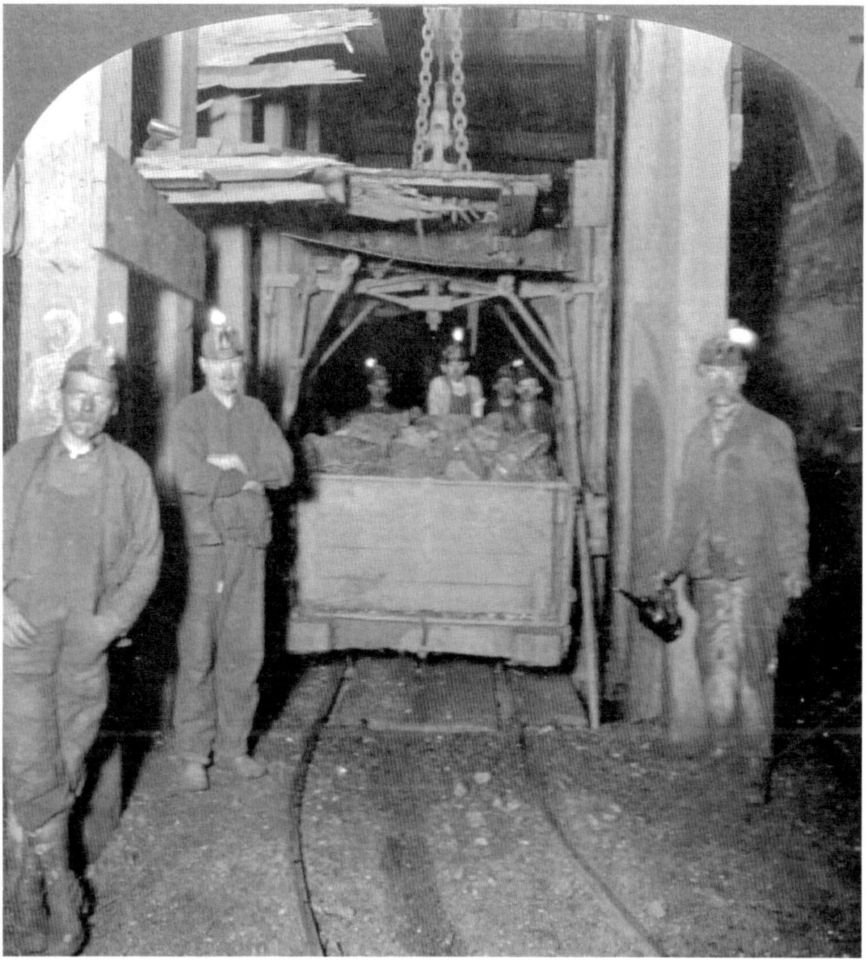

Miners standing in a loading cage next to a full car of coal waiting to be dumped into the breaker.

under piles of legislation and a government that didn't want to get involved unless a strike threatened coal production. It took about fifteen years for the broken Knights of Labor to join up with the equally downtrodden National Federation of Miners to become the United Mine Workers of America in 1890. This union tried itself out at first by going up against the coal operators in the Midwest and western Pennsylvania for safer working conditions, and it won. The UMWA's success rate did decline for the next ten years as it tried to stay as practical as possible, with its goals being to get "proper earnings" and safer working conditions. Part of the group's problem was that a large number of its members were midwestern and western bituminous miners, and the largest number of miners were working in the anthracite fields.

When John Mitchell became the president of UMWA in 1899, he had to deal with years upon years of road blocks that people like Terence V. Powderly and Samuel Gompers had tried desperately to work through but were still held back by coal operators. He decided early on to travel east, and in 1900, he came to organize in Pennsylvania. He and his organizers, who included longtime labor advocate Mother Jones, went directly to the dusty, poverty-ridden camps and towns that the miners lived in and tried to convince as many miners as possible about the benefits of joining a union. He even urged the miners to forget the difference of their ethnicities: "The coal you dig isn't Slavish or Polish, or Irish coal. It's just coal." With Mitchell's wise words and passion for helping the miners rise up and fight for their rights without being too radical, many priests and preachers supported him and his cause and even became union organizers.

After successfully organizing in Pennsylvania, Mitchell attempted to gain a foothold against the anthracite coal operators of northeastern Pennsylvania, but unlike the operators in the bituminous area of the country, the operators in Pennsylvania were "as hard as the coal they mined." After multiple attempts to get the operators to discuss ways to solve the grievances of the miners in which he was virtually ignored by George F. Baer, who was president of the Philadelphia and Reading Railroad and spoke for the operators, Mitchell called his newly organized men to strike.

THE STRIKE OF 1900

Even though the 1900 strike was short-lived and only lasted about six weeks, it was the first time that Mitchell and Baer went up against each other. Sadly, Mitchell had the misfortune of striking during an election year when William McKinley was up for reelection. Whenever a president of the United States got involved with any kind of labor situation in the nineteenth century, it was usually as strikebreaker. In 1834, Andrew Jackson sent troops to construction sites of the Chesapeake and Ohio Canal, and during the violence of the 1877 rail strikes, Rutherford B. Hayes sent out troops to prevent "obstruction of the mails." Even Grover Cleveland made use of soldiers during the 1894 Pullman strikes.

With the threat of losing voters for his campaign, McKinley was concerned but did not get directly involved in the proceedings to stop the strike. Instead his campaign manager, Senator Marcus Hanna, spoke with the famous Wall Street financier J.P. Morgan, who also had a lot to lose from the strike because he owned railroads, which included the railroad operated by George Baer. Also, Morgan had recently bought land in the anthracite region, where he owned debt on the railroads. If the strike was to go on for longer, he was looking to lose a large quantity of money.

With pressure from Morgan and the Republican Party, Baer and the other operators backed down and gave a 10 percent increase to the miners' wages, and the strike was immediately called off. The outcome for this strike didn't fix all the problems of the miners, and UMWA still wasn't recognized as a union by the operators; however, in a landscape of people who looked down on miners and the people trying to help them, Mitchell considered the 1900 strike as his first major victory—not to mention that McKinley won the election, and Morgan's finances were still on the rise without the threat of losing anything on the anthracite coal fields. Almost everyone involved in the strike was happy with its outcome—except for, of course, the pressured coal operators. Baer and his associates thought they were forced to concede and decided that if they were ever contested again, they would stand their ground and not give in to the union.

THE LEAD UP TO 1902

It didn't take long for trouble to start again or for the UMWA to launch into its second standoff with Baer and the operators. In between 1900 and 1902, the coal operators had frequently violated their contract to increase the miners' wages. This created an uproar in the ranks of the UMWA with Mother Jones and other organizers, who risked their lives by trying to organize the union daily. They demanded that Mitchell call another strike since the operators were not cooperating with something they were legally bound to do.

Mitchell did not want another strike at all and tried everything in his power to prevent it from happening. He thought it would be better if the public saw that the labor group was holding to its side of the bargain to try to sway them to sympathize with the laboring class instead of the coal barons. In March of that year, Mitchell, along with anthracite laborers, established new demands for the operators that included a 20 percent increase in wages, an eight- instead of ten-hour workday, a system of openly weighing coal and paying for it by the actual tonnage instead of by the cartload and recognition of UMWA as a union. By April 1, 1902, the contract had finally run out, and Mitchell invited the operators to renegotiate with his new terms in a joint conference. His invitation was ignored.

Mitchell tried to give the operators the benefit of the doubt, and since he did not want to call another strike, he went to Senator Hanna for help. At the time, Hanna was the president of the National Civic Federation (NCF), which was an organization founded in 1900 that specifically tried to settle disputes between "capital and labor." Mitchell was also a member of the NCF, and he and Hanna had become strong friends since the 1900 strike. Hanna, as he did the first time, tried to find a peaceful way to get the operators to cooperate and called the representatives of both parties to meet in New York to discuss the best course of action to renegotiate the contract. After Mitchell laid out the terms that the miners wanted, Baer and the operators refused to be humiliated once more by Mitchell and Hanna and did not agree to the terms. Thirty days later, Hanna and Mitchell tried to work with the operators once more but were, again, ignored.

Because Mitchell did not push for union recognition during the 1900 strike and since the operators were no longer cooperating, they were essentially back to square one, with Mitchell in a tight spot and nowhere else to move. On May 12, 1902, he called 147,000 workers to the anthracite mines, and thus the "Great Strike" began.

THE SIX-MONTH STRIKE

During the spring, summer and fall of 1902, the UMWA and the anthracite coal operators were gridlocked on where to go next, as neither one would concede to the terms of the other. During this time period, Mother Jones and other organizers would go from mine town to mine town to make sure that the union mine workers were staying out of the mines. Deprived of their normal income, these thousands of miners were forced to cut back almost entirely on what little they had for food. The union treasury did try to support them with what it had, but that was still on a "bare subsistence level"; some families were forced to live on just bread and water when things became desperate. Many were forced to relocate. Out of the 147,000, 30,000 left the region, and of that number 8,000 to 10,000 returned to Europe.

During this time, John Mitchell was determined to keep the strike as nonviolent as possible to once again garner support from the public and also from the NCF, business leaders and political bosses. Many of the miners complied, but as the weather got warmer, so did the tempers of the jobless miners who were getting replaced by nonunion workers, otherwise known by the derogatory terms "scabs" or "black-legs," just so the operators could keep their mines open. This proved inefficient as most of these workers lacked the skills of experienced miners, and in late May, when the UMWA called out the mine maintenance workers—the firemen and engineers who were in charge of the pumps that kept the mines from flooding—the operators had no experienced workers to replace them.

This was the most serious threat to the operators because without these workers or if the job was left to a "green hand," the mines could easily be flooded and it would take an estimated sixteen months to get the mine in working order again.

The operators weren't giving in that easily, though, and countered by enlisting five thousand coal and iron police, turning their mines into armed camps, where the "hired guns" patrolled night and day. The operators also made absolutely sure that their troops of police were legitimatized by Pennsylvania's state legislature. "For one dollar each, coal and steel operators could have the governor sign commissions and the Police were endowed with all the powers of the law to enforce the companies' interests." Many of these men were unemployed thugs from New York City and Philadelphia, and their rough dispositions mixed with their general lack of discipline exasperated an already volatile situation.

From the end of May through most of June, the strikers and the coal and iron police were constantly going toe to toe with one another. In Pittston, a mob of miners retaliated on the coal and iron police when they attacked a ten-year-old boy who was teasing the police. The strikers crowded around the colliery and attacked the policemen. They ended up badly hurting John Williams, the superintendent of the Erie Colliery. The first rifle shots of the strike went off soon after at the Empire Colliery of the Lehigh and Wilkes-Barre Coal Company as police on guard were trying to drive back a mob of men and boy strikers who wanted to burn the colliery down. Nobody was hit or injured during that altercation as the fired shots dispersed them.

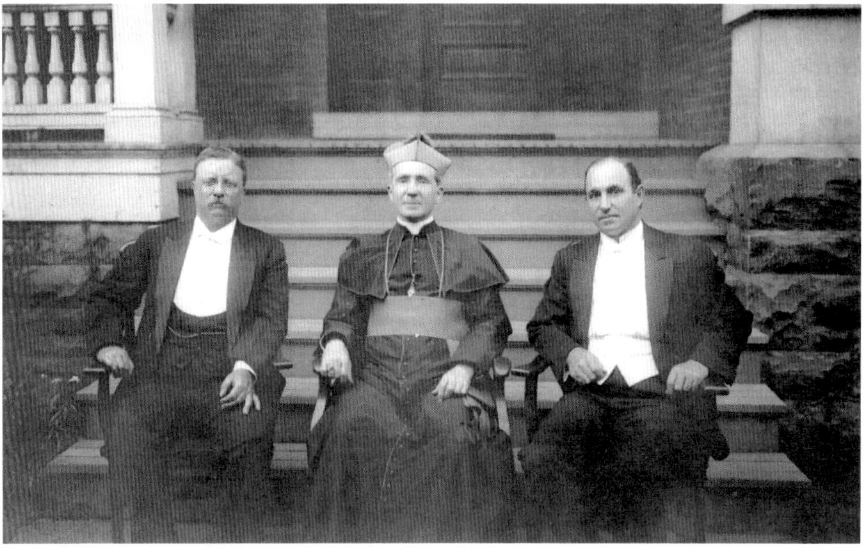

From left to right: President Theodore Roosevelt, Bishop Hoban and Johnny Mitchell. The photo was taken at a local society function in 1910. *Courtesy of the Pennsylvania Historical and Museum Commission.*

Besides trying to drive back the coal and iron police, the strikers started to harass the men who still chose to work at the mines during the strike. There was an incident at Miner's Mill when a group of strikers spotted several men who lived nearby and were engineers and pump men at the Dorrance and Pine Ridge collieries. At the time, many workers chose to sleep in barracks located at the mines because they were protected by the coal and iron police. The few men whom the strikers spotted decided to take a chance and go home for the night. They were immediately stopped by the imposing crowd of miners but escaped any act of humiliation or violence by promising not to attempt to go back to work again.

The same strikers at Miner's Mill weren't finished after they were able to stop some nonunion men from going to work. They went on and prepared a "stuffed figure" that had a sign attached to it with a threat against the men who were still at work. They carried the figure at the head of their line as they marched to the houses of nonunion workers. As they stopped in front of each house, it was reported that the strikers' fife and drum corps started to play a death march while the Welsh miners in the crowd sang a dirge in their native tongue. Besides the morbid singing and marching, another scare tactic was the hanging of effigies that the strikers tried to keep up at any means necessary. For example, a group of Italian strikers in Duryea forced a

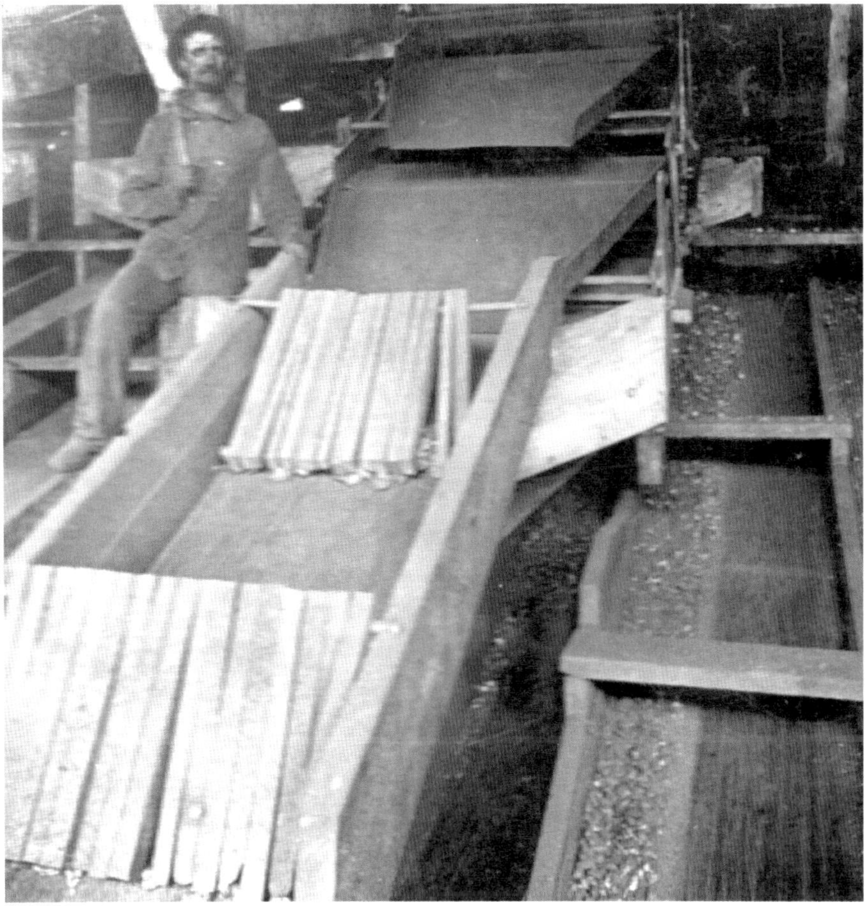

The Tandem Automatic Slate Picker later replaced the breaker boys. Other machines were invented to make child labor unnecessary in the mine.

telephone repair gang to rehang effigies back onto the telephone poles from which the telephone men had previously taken them.

Not all of the strikers' threats were quite so entertaining. Soon the strikers began to call the homes of the nonunion workers and threatened the wives of the miners that they were going to blow up their homes with dynamite, and in one dangerous incident in Plymouth, it was reported that an attack was made on a group of nonunion men who were trying to board a train that was going to take them to the mine. Hundreds of men, women and children tried to block the nonunion men from getting on the train, while children threw stones at them. A fight broke out immediately among the crowd with everyone getting involved in the brawl. The coal and iron police tried to rescue the nonunion workers but were "roughly handled" by the strikers. When the fight ended, two rioters were arrested and several men were injured.

As noted before, the UMWA frowned on the use of violence to get its point across, but it seems that most of these incidents and ones that followed in the succeeding months were either spontaneously brought about or led by "informal" strike leaders. The UMWA tried desperately to keep any more of these violent outbursts from happening, and in one case, J.P. Gallagher, who was the district secretary of the UMWA, made sure that five kidnapped coal and iron policemen were returned home. These five policemen were captured at a railroad station when they arrived in Philadelphia. Gallagher made sure transportation was provided for them so they could return home safely.

What did help both the striking miners and the UMWA was Pennsylvania's rainy weather. The strikers believed that after a heavy rainfall followed by hot weather, the "green hands" in the fire rooms and the engines wouldn't be able to handle the flush of water through the pipes or the heat in the fire rooms and would be forced to quit.

During June, either from heavy rains or workers breaking the pumps, many mines began to flood, just as the striking workmen had hoped, forcing the operators to close down the mines until they could be repaired. Some of these floods were in the Avondale mine, where one of the worst mining disasters in history occurred. This mine flooded in June, and there was even a threat of an imminent cave-in, forcing the workers and the coal and iron police to depart immediately. The No. 11 of the Lehigh and Wilkes-Barre Company was offering five dollars a day for any unskilled workers. This offer was made in vain as the unskilled workers who stood in for the all-important pump men accidentally broke the pumps, flooding the mine. At the No. 5 of the Susquehanna Coal Company in Nanticoke, shafts flooded, and there was the added danger of gas accumulating in the mine. Matters became so dangerous at the No. 5 that warning notices had to be posted.

Another disaster that was common with the miners before the strike was the threat of a fire in the mines. Seventy men hired by the DL&W to fight a fire that raged on at the Jersey Mine up and quit when strikers made their lives miserable. In the same area, a nonunion man's house was mysteriously burned, and there were reports of the miners' wives getting threats on their own homes.

Also in June, operators tried some inventive ways to defend their collieries from the oncoming strikers, as reported in a local paper:

> *Huge photographic cameras and heavy loads of flashlight powders are to be installed as a part of the defenses of Fort Susquehanna at Nanticoke. Colliery No. 5, at Nanticoke, or Fort Susquehanna, as it is called, has been fortified and garrisoned by the operators in a manner truly military and is in the charge of a young lieutenant, who served in the Cuban campaign, and who is a graduate of Yale. He has provided for the protection of the colliery in a manner to excite the admiration of military authorities and now to the barbed wire entanglements, moats and stockades with eighty armed men and a thousand feet of heavy fire hose, he has added a battery of cameras. It is the intention of Lieutenant Jones to have several professional photographers in readiness at the colliery to take a number of photographs of any crowd that attempts to make an attack of any sort on the coal fort.*

Costs of this protection, along with the costs of fixing a flooding mine or a mine in need of rebuilding, became a pretty hefty sum. It is figured that the strike was costing the operators more than $250,000 each week, and that is only the money the superintendents admitted that they lost. The other losses of the coal operators and their companies can only be guessed at, but since coal production was at an all-time minimum—nonunion workers were quitting daily—it is estimated by local newspapers at the time that $2 million in total was lost during the strike.

As July and August rolled in, patience began to thin for both sides of the fight, and the relative peace that defined the beginning of the strike was broken. Many of the unionist miners had grown tired of living on little food and having no prospects of a future, for the strike was still stuck in the same place it had been when it began. These frustrated miners began to return to work, whether the men still striking wanted them to or not. The solidarity between the striking miners began to crumble, as did their will to play nice with the nonunion workers. A mob in Silver Brook kidnapped a scab worker named Rudolph Hensel. After his capture, they made him walk five miles in the rain to McAdoo, where he was paraded through the streets at the head of the mob and made to kneel in the mud at the corner of Blain and Logan Streets to pray for fifteen minutes. Afterward, he was released to go home, but this marked a change in the intimidation tactics of the strikers that proved to have a violent effect later on.

On July 2, the coal and iron police fired their guns to ward off a striker once more, but this time, they hit and killed him. They claimed that he didn't listen to them when he tried to climb a fence after being ordered to stop. This set off another violent chain of events for the strikers, and three hundred of

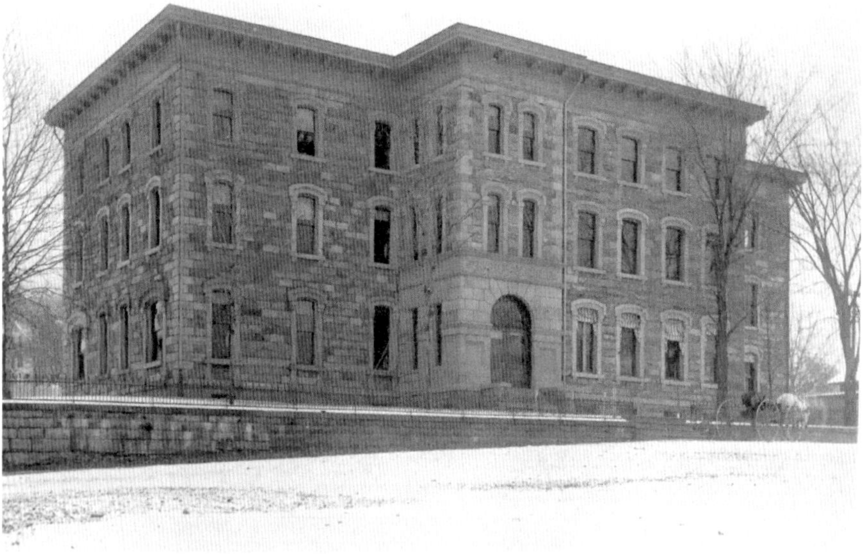

The offices of the Pennsylvania Coal Company were located in Dunmore, Pennsylvania.

them attacked another train carrying workers and police to the mines. The men inside had to dive to the ground as the strikers hurled rocks at the train's windows and fired their guns. One of the most infamous and disastrous incidents of the 1902 strike happened in Shenandoah on July 30. A mob of angered strikers attacked a deputy sheriff who was escorting nonunion men into a colliery, and the deputy was forced to hide in the Reading Railroad depot. The deputy's brother tried to smuggle arms into the depot, but he was caught by the mob and beaten to death. The deputy and the nonunion men were able to escape. Later the county sheriff contacted the Pennsylvania governor at the time, William A. Stone, and he sent more than three thousand men of the National Guard into the coal fields, headed by Brigadier General John Gobin, who issued the order of "shoot to kill" for any striker who tried to "assault them."

As union officials became infuriated at the way the situation was being handled and demanded that the National Guard be removed, the guard proved to only aggravate matters and did nothing to quell the violence and destruction of the strikers. Even Scranton had problems from the miners:

Today an engineer in West Scranton had to draw a revolver to defend himself. When the young men engaged in stoning him saw the weapon drawn they walked off. Trains carrying washery coal are being stoned regularly as they pass through the "Notch," a wild suburb of Scranton. Last night on the Winton branch of the Lackawanna road an effort was made to dynamite a train of coal. One of the great hog engines was drawing this train. The dynamite shook it up but failed to knock it from the train.

Toward the end of August, the strike evolved into a fight of what the public saw between the operators and the miners. The operators were determined to prove that everything was going well in the mines and that they were resuming production, while the strikers tried and

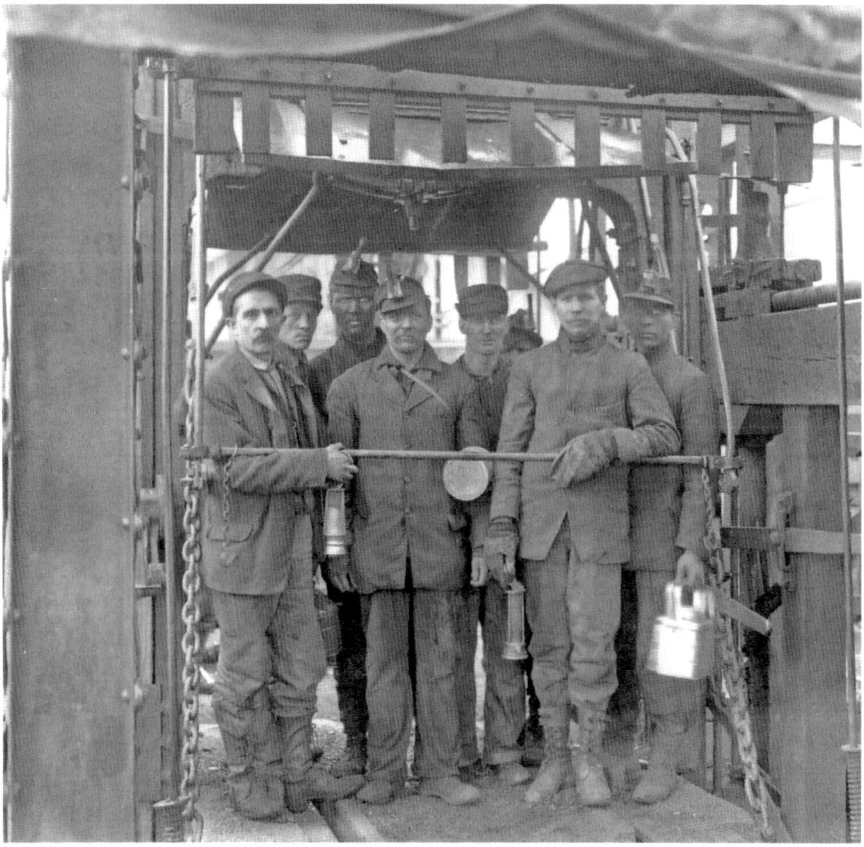

Some Pennsylvania shafts were sunk three thousand feet beneath the earth's surface, which meant some of the coal was mined below sea level, resulting in the need for pumps to keep the water from flooding the mine.

succeeded in proving that the exact opposite was going on. On August 27, the Klondike colliery, which was owned and operated by Joseph G. Saeger, burned to the ground. The colliery had been trying to operate for two weeks even with the protestors trying to bang down its doors. This colliery even had a permit from the UMWA to remain active, but a week before the fire, strikers drove off the workmen of the mine. It was reopened the day before the incident, but again the mob returned to drive away the workers. An alarm was immediately sounded when the flames were discovered, and hundreds of men and boys ran to the site. Not one of them raised a hand to stop the complete destruction of the breaker, which cost the company $8,000.

In September, times grew even more desperate, and as the violence increased, so did the strength of the Pennsylvania National Guard, growing to ten thousand. With many of these soldiers coming from the working class themselves, they naturally were sympathetic to the strikers, and there were reports of incidents of soldiers trying to help the strikers. In Scranton, on September 24, a sergeant and a private were drummed out of camp for assaulting two nonunion men. Their uniforms were taken from them, and they left the camp wearing overalls. As they walked over the camp's line, they were immediately arrested for assault and battery.

These reports and examples of incidents during the coal mine strike of 1902 are not even half of what happened at the time, and since newspapers were always more willing to track the "ferocity" of the striking miners and their rebel union leaders instead of what the coal and iron police and the operators were up to, it is hard to give a definitive answer on who was in the wrong during the full six months of the strike. It seems, in this case, that it is possible to blame both equally, as each side retaliated to the other with usually more force until the National Guard left the coal fields on October 24. When it comes down to it, it is nearly impossible to truly know what happened unless you were there to experience it yourself.

When the threat of a coal-less winter in Pennsylvania loomed on the horizon in October and the destruction of property went so far as strikers dynamiting a nonunion worker's house to pieces, President Theodore Roosevelt called for a meeting that would truly change the way labor issues were handled by the U.S. government.

THE WRIGHT REPORT

President Roosevelt was actually interested in the 1902 strike long before he called the attention of the operators and the UMWA for the unprecedented meeting in October. It started for him on June 8, when he asked Carroll D. Wright, the commissioner of labor, to investigate what was going on at the anthracite coal fields and then report back to him.

Wright thought it was best not to go directly to the coal fields because he thought that a representative of the president would add more fuel to the already growing fire on the fields, so he headed to New York City, where he interviewed people like independent mine operators, financiers, presidents of coal roads, superintendents and mine foremen. He was also able to get John Mitchell to New York so they could talk about the miners' side of the issue.

In twelve days' time, he sent the report by a special courier to the president to be reviewed. According to Jonathan Grossman in his article "The Coal Strike of 1902—Turning Point in U.S. Policy," "Wright reported that both parties cooperated with his investigation and that sharply different opinions arose out of different positions and not out of misrepresentation." He was able to reduce the "highly emotional" claims down to the bare-bones facts, and he observed that there were more "varying conditions, conflicting views, and irritating complaints than any he had encountered." He went on to

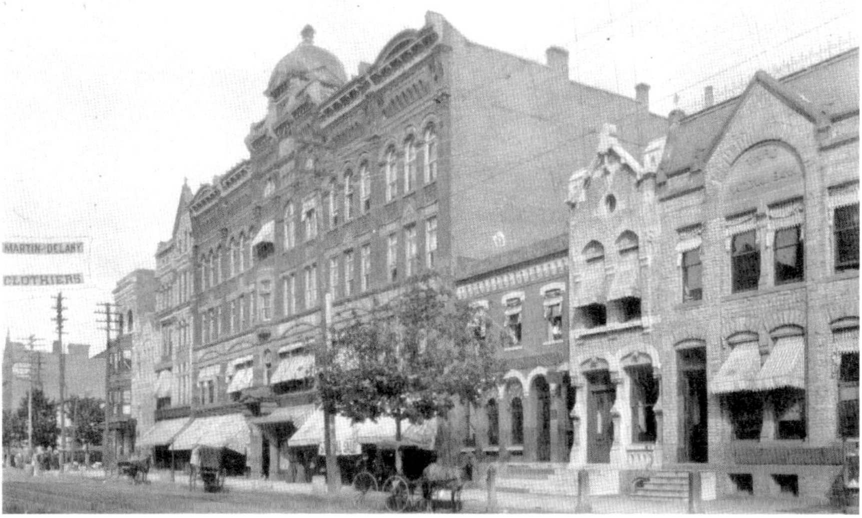

The Coal Exchange building opened in 1885. It was one of the first office buildings in Scranton.

explain how the strike began, what the workers demanded, the complaints and the claims of the employers, the dispute over how coal was weighed, the miners' wages, the cost of production and its profits—just to name a few.

Wright even added in his own suggestions on terms that would be beneficial for both the miners and the operators: "He proposed an experimental reduction from 10 to 9 hours a day, protection of nonunion men, a joint committee on conciliation, and wherever practicable, collective bargaining." Wright himself knew that these suggestions would not solve every problem for both sides but thought that they could at least be a step forward in the realm of labor rights.

Wright's report made it seem as if the strike could be settled early on, and the strikers themselves were eager for it to be published. There was a little snag, though, because while President Roosevelt liked the report, he didn't want the publishing of the report to be seen as approval of Wright's recommendations when he wasn't yet ready to make a decided commitment.

Newspapers immediately jumped on this and claimed that the president didn't want to publish the report because the terms were in favor of the miners, and while Wright vehemently denied the accusation, President Roosevelt was troubled by the charge and so decided to make the report public in August.

A MEETING WITH CAPITAL AND LABOR

With the publication and a definite plan of terms being brought to the table, Theodore Roosevelt sent telegrams to both sides of the strike, this the intention of holding a meeting on October 3 in Washington. This was an invitation that the operators could not ignore. As stated before, it was unprecedented for a president to get involved in labor issues. Even McKinley wasn't truly involved with the 1900 strike; it was Senator Hanna who presided over the terms of that agreement. But Roosevelt threw his whole self into the idea of coming to an agreement that would benefit both parties to save the nation from an economic collapse and a fuel famine.

The meeting was held at 22 Lafayette Square. Baer spoke for the coal operators; John Markle, the head of the G.B. Markle and Company firm, spoke for the independent operators; and, of course, John Mitchell spoke for the laborers. At the time, President Roosevelt was still convalescing from an accident he had the month before when his carriage was hit by a trolley

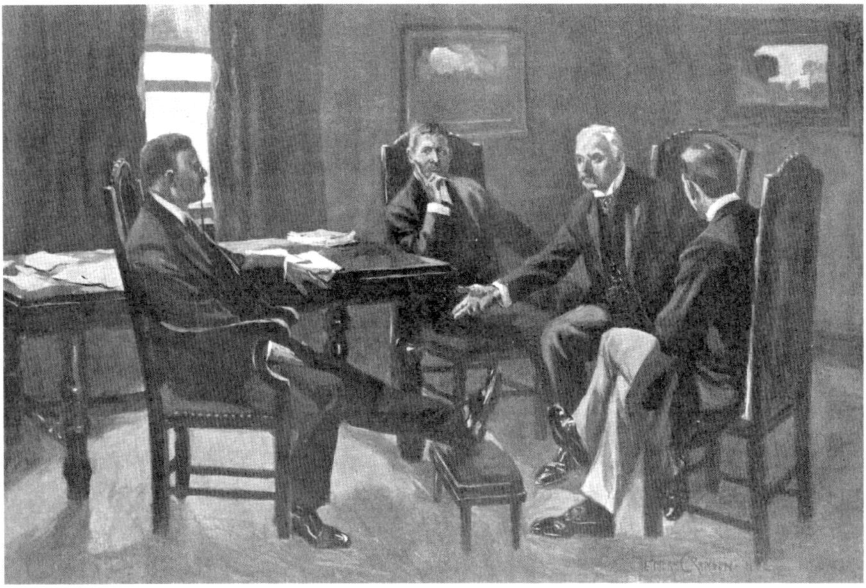

The end of the coal strike is near. The conference—held on October 13, 1902, in the White House between President Roosevelt, J. Pierpont Morgan and other coal barons—is considered epic in the history of relations between labor and capital.

car, so throughout the meeting, he sat in a wheelchair but still managed to control the room with his commanding voice. He pleaded with all parties to bring the situation to an end by making "individual sacrifices" in the name of patriotism and "for the greater good."

Mitchell quickly replied that a committee, to be selected by the president, should be formed and agreed upon to look at the issues at hand and then come to an agreement, but Baer and Markle both seethed at the idea, with Markle telling the president that only military action could bring the strike to an end and Baer flat out insulting the president by calling the U.S. government a "contemptible failure" if it could protect lives and property only by compromising with "violators of law and the instigators of violence and crime." He also went on to argue that Roosevelt should do everything in his power to protect the people who wanted to work instead of trying to deal with the striking laborers. Needless to say, the meeting failed to resolve the strike.

WHAT THE PEOPLE THOUGHT

When Roosevelt, Mitchell and Baer began an almost month-long battle as to how to come to terms with one another, the media was having a field day with the news that the beloved Teddy Roosevelt was throwing himself into the fray of labor disputes. President Roosevelt was known for overcoming obstacles through nothing more than sheer willpower. He even overcame his own health problems of asthma and nearsightedness to become a champion boxer when he attended Harvard. In the mid-nineteenth century, he moved to a ranch in a part of North Dakota called the Badlands and befriended the ranchers and farmers, which probably made him more sympathetic to what the UMWA was going through. Roosevelt personally enforced the law when he was the president of New York's Board of Police Commissioners, and when he eventually became president in 1901, he was already fully prepared to meet the threat that a coal strike posed to American citizens. He thought of himself as "the steward of the people" and was more than willing to impose himself into the middle of the strike because he knew that he would do whatever it took to resolve the problem.

Roosevelt was one of the most "media-savvy" presidents at the time as well and knew the importance of letting the public know just exactly what he was willing to do, so while it was uncalled for at the time for a president to get so deeply involved with a strike, it was almost the status quo for Roosevelt, who was always up for a new challenge.

Mitchell also gained a lot of attention and always seemed to be the center of any of the strike stories. Like Roosevelt, he understood how important the thoughts of the public were and seemed to know the perfectly calculated way to speak, dress and approach the American people. Mitchell was known for his conservative appearance; he dressed "in the manner of a priest" and was clean shaven like most Roman Catholic priests of the time period. He wanted to come across as different from how the public might think a labor leader would look and be like. He was obviously passionate about the rights of the workingman, but he didn't want to be thought of as violent, uneducated and dirty, as some of the strikers and their predecessors were considered. Because he was the public face of the UMWA, Mitchell knew that he had to be adaptable and always willing to compromise, and even if he couldn't compromise, he tried his best to stay respectful, even under the fire and brimstone of the operators.

One of the more surprising factors in this strike was that throughout, the public seemed to stay on the side of the strikers and did not sympathize with

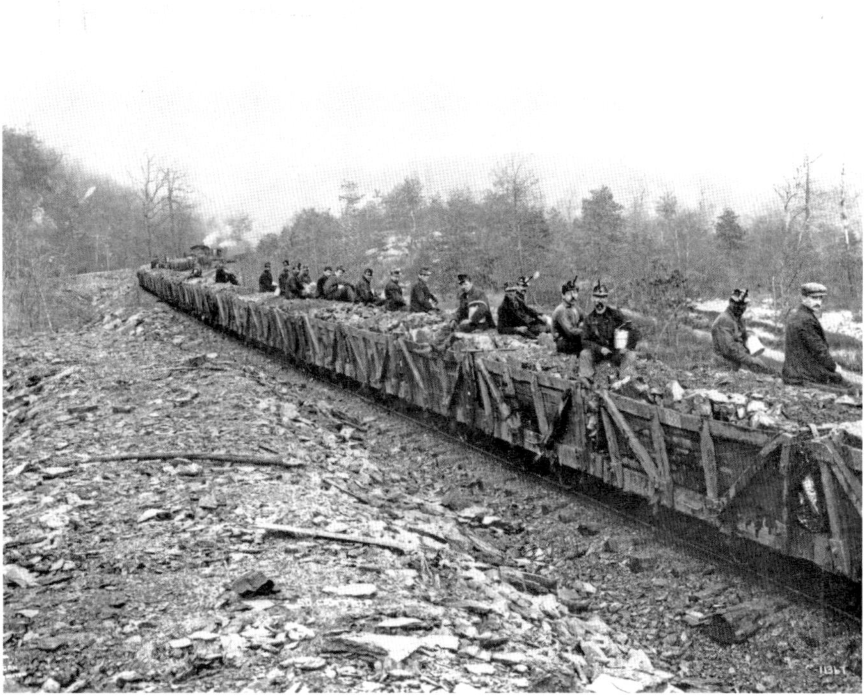

Miners photographed on a coal train.

the operators, whom they had sympathized with only a few years before. This, in part, was due to the burgeoning Progressive movement that was gaining steam throughout the strike, and more and more unfair business practices of the "fat cat" capitalist were coming into a stark light that revealed to the nation what an American aristocrat was really like. It also didn't help that Baer was as tactless as he was arrogant and downright rude. One of the turning points in the struggle for popular opinion came when Baer gave, in a letter to a clergyman in Wilkes-Barre, what was later to be known as his "Divine Right" speech, in which he stated that the capitalists had a "God-given right to manage their property as they saw fit." Instead of running to his side, the public was shocked by Baer's arrogance and ignorance and flocked to the side of labor.

It most certainly did not help that Baer was openly confrontational with the much-loved president of the United States either. He and the operators only dug themselves into a deeper grave.

FORMING THE ARBITRATION COMMISSION

Roosevelt did blame the operators for their stubborn inactiveness to a point, but being well aware of the fights between the police and the strikers, he knew he could not put the labor side up on a pedestal. Because he knew that the operators were not willing to budge whatsoever, he appealed to the open-minded Mitchell on October 6 to end the strike, and if the miners went back to work, the president would reward the UMWA by setting up a commission to investigate the matters at hand and come to a conclusion that would help the miners.

Mitchell learned his lesson from the 1900 strike and knew that the operators would not honor any agreement where the miners conceded first. When he put the idea to a vote with the miners, they all voted to keep the strike going and refused to surrender or sacrifice any more than they already had.

Since both sides of the fight were not complying whatsoever and it didn't seem like the strike would ever end, President Roosevelt showed his last hand. He threatened both parties with an order for the U.S. Army to take control of the coal fields. This decision would have ended up hurting both the strikers and the operators, as it would interfere with the striking miners

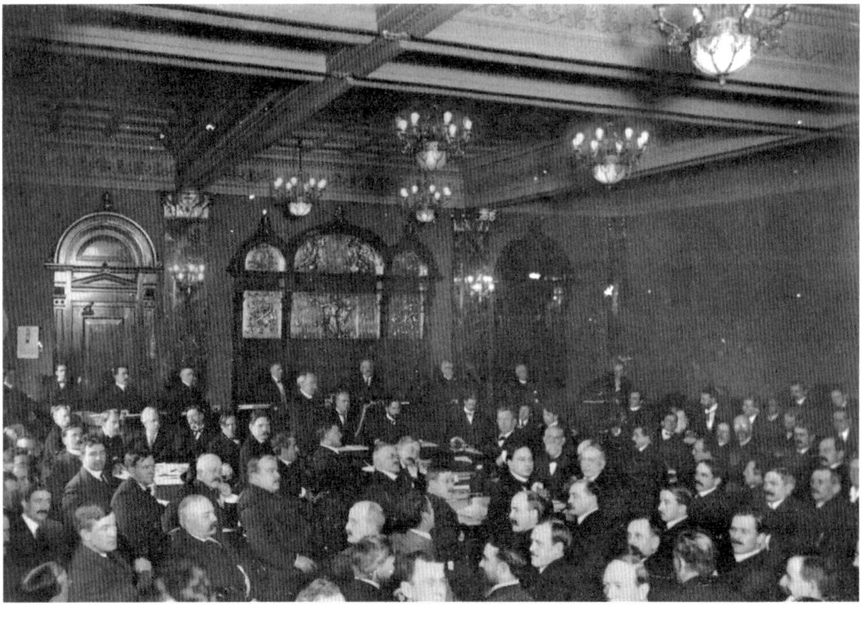

The Anthracite Coal Strike Commission in session at Scranton, Pennsylvania, on November 17, 1902.

if they ever wanted to resume their work and it would mean that the army would "run the mines" no matter what God-given right Baer and the other operators thought they had.

This time both sides conceded, but it wasn't exactly amicably. On October 13, Secretary of War Elihu Root brought an arbitration proposal to President Roosevelt that he and his friend J.P. Morgan had written on Morgan's yacht, where the "newspaper reporters could not bother them." The proposal was for the end of the strike and the miners' return to work while an arbitration committee "considered the issues." This, of course, was nothing new, but Root and Morgan added something to entice the operators into complying: "Each company and its own employees would present their differences to the commission. This would spare the operators from dealing directly with the miners' union and show the public that the coal industry would arbitrate with its workers."

By this time, the price of coal was skyrocketing to twenty dollars per ton, and the operators were beginning to fall into deep financial trouble. Obviously they weren't starving as many of the miners were at the time, but they were embarrassed to see that the union was ready and willing to outlast them until the bitter end. Seeing this, and with the added pressure of J.P. Morgan once again weighing on their minds, the coal operators finally relented to the arbitration committee, but only if one condition was met: "They demanded that the president set up the committee composed of five men—a military engineer, a mining engineer, a judge, an expert in the coal business, and an 'eminent sociologist.' The list just so happened to lack anyone to be in favor of the laborers."

Mitchell was more than a little alarmed at the thought of a stacked committee and the fact that the operators were still refusing to recognize the union or that he was its president. He knew better than to force the union issue but wanted the president to add a "labor man" who understood the point of view of the miners and a Roman Catholic priest because a large population of the miners were Catholic. Roosevelt understood and agreed to pick his own people for the commission.

One of the more comedic portions of this back-and-forth battle on who would be on the commission board was just whom Roosevelt picked to represent the laborer since the operators, once again, refused to have a "labor man" on the board. To get around this, all Roosevelt had to do was appoint E.E. Clark, who was the head of the railway conductors' union, as the "eminent sociologist" when, in actuality, he was the person whom Roosevelt wanted for the "labor man."

This time, because Roosevelt gave Clark a different title, the operators agreed, and they even agreed to add a Catholic bishop. On October 16, the arbitration committee was fully formed and consisted of Clark, Bishop John Spalding, Judge George Gray (who became the elected chairman), Edward Parker, Thomas Watkins and Brigadier General John Wilson. Originally, Carroll Wright was supposed to be assigned as the recorder, but the committee ended up voting him in as a full member. With that, the arbitration committee was underway.

Once the committee was fully formed and approved, the Great Strike of 1902 was called off by Mitchell on October 23. In full, the strike lasted 163 days, and there were seven recorded deaths during that time. Even with the numerous stories of the riotous strikers and the undisciplined coal and iron police, the strike was known as being one of the most organized in American history. After the National Guard was fully out of the region by the end of the month, the violence ceased while everyone waited with bated breath to see what conclusion the commission would come to.

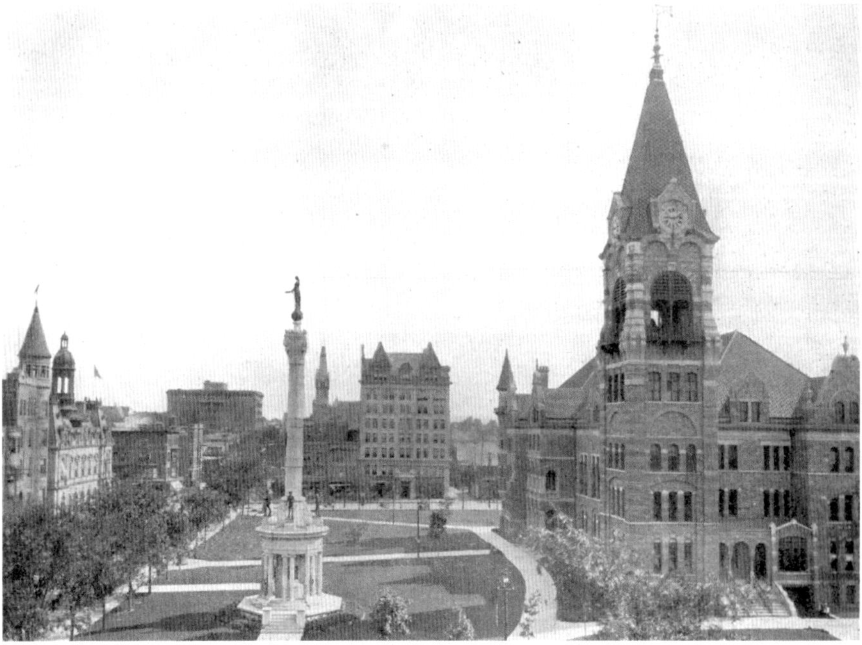

The Lackawanna County Courthouse is where the hearings of the 1902 Anthracite Coal Strike Commission commenced in November of the same year.

After a brief powwow in Washington on the twenty-fourth, when official pictures were taken and the future sessions scheduled, they settled down for lunch with the president before beginning the gargantuan task of settling a "Great Strike."

The Arbitration Committee Meetings

The commission meetings first started when the commissioners spent a week in the coal fields, getting a firsthand tour of where the miners lived and worked. Grossman states that after the inspection, they met for nearly three months of committee sessions that were held at the Lackawanna County Courthouse in Scranton. During these meetings

> *five-hundred fifty-eight witnesses appeared, including 240 for the striking miners, 153 for non-union mineworkers and 154 for the operators. The Commission itself requested the appearance of 11 witnesses. The testimony ran to 10,047 legal-sized pages in addition to other exhibits. John Mitchell played a prominent role in presenting the case for the miners. George Baer made the closing arguments for the coal operators, while Clarence Darrow closed for the workers.*

By the end of the three months, the commissioners came to a conclusion that while some cases of miners' conditions were considered terrible, for the most part, conditions were good for the miners and they were only "partly justified in their claim that annual earnings were not sufficient 'to maintain an American standard of living.'" The commissioners then split the difference for the original terms that UMWA asked for and gave workers a 10 percent wage increase and a nine-hour workday. No matter what, the operators still refused to recognize the UMWA, and coal was still to be paid by the cartload.

Mitchell seemed to be more or less content with the decision, but members of the UMWA argued with him over the terms. The most vocal of them was Mother Jones, who believed that Mitchell was "overawed" by the president and needed to stand his ground to get the recognition they still desperately needed. She proposed that Mitchell force the owners to "sit down face to face with labor leaders" and finish what they had been fighting for for years.

Mitchell respectfully disagreed with Mother Jones's claims, and on March 22, 1903, he agreed to the results of the arbitration.

Some consider this a hollow victory and thought, as Mother Jones did, that Mitchell gave in too early, not holding out for some of the more important demands. Others, including Mitchell himself, thought that the strike of 1902 was one of the biggest successes in Pennsylvania labor history, a breakthrough after decades of struggles and tragedies, including the riot on Lackawanna Avenue in 1877 and the Lattimer Massacre of 1897.

In a way, the strike can be seen in both lights. It is possible that Mitchell could have asked for more, denied the president or pushed the operators and the miners to a more violent breaking point—by which time more than seven people would have perished in the process—but Mitchell knew that government was more of a chess match than a war zone. He decided that even to get the operators to comply a little bit was more than nothing and that later on there were always more games to play than battles to be won. He understood the importance of playing by someone else's rules to get what

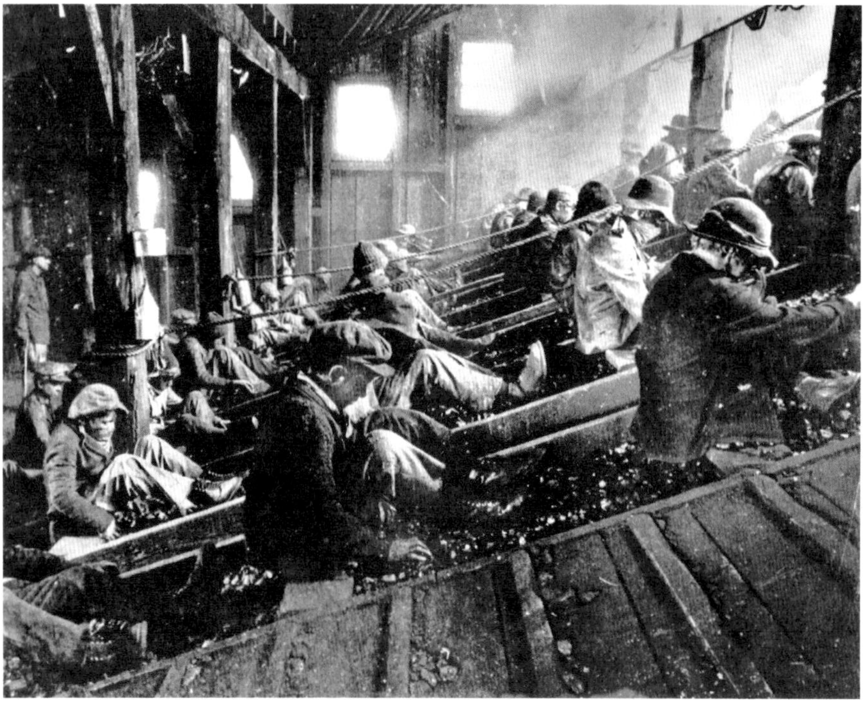

Breaker boys sat all day long in a cramped space beside the small coal chute working for a small sum of money.

was needed instead of showing overblown vehemence. In this situation, his negotiations worked nearly as well as he had planned, and though it would still take years before the UMWA was recognized as a union, the strike was a definite victory on the side of progress. The success of the Great Strike of 1902 opened the nation's mind to the idea that laborers could fight for their liberty and their freedom again.

5
THE LEGACY

In most strikes that occurred during the late nineteenth century, the U.S. government did not intervene. President Theodore Roosevelt's involvement in the coal strike of 1902 set a new precedent in the relationship between government and labor. Roosevelt's intervention worked to his political advantage; his new reputation of standing up to the coal barons helped him to easily win the presidential election in 1904. But there were other long-term effects of the strike, and they were just as important. The federal government now acted in a more neutral manner in business-labor disputes. This eventually led to increased regulation, such as the Hepburn Act and the Pure Food and Drug Act.

However, it would be many years before the union won protection and recognition by the federal government. Most agree the strike of 1902, with Teddy Roosevelt's involvement, was the turning point as well as the basis for other changes in the labor movement.

THE PENNSYLVANIA STATE POLICE

As a direct result of the 1902 Strike Commission report, the Pennsylvania State Police was created as an executive department of the state government by Senate Bill 278, which was signed into law by Governor Samuel W. Pennypacker on May 2, 1905. The governmental department became the first uniformed police organization of its kind in the nation. Not surprisingly, the department was opposed by many because organized labor and others feared that the state police would be utilized as a private army.

Their duty was to patrol Pennsylvania's forty-five thousand square miles. The department was divided into four troops: Troop A (Greensburg), Troop B (Wilkes-Barre, later moved to Wyoming), Troop C (Reading) and Troop D (Punxsutawney).

The four troops helped control mob violence, patrol farm areas and protect wildlife and assisted in tracking and capturing criminals. Their excellent work ethics did not take long to change the public's opinion, and the state police soon gained a reputation for fairness and honesty.

John Charles Groome was the first commissioner of the Pennsylvania State Police; he served from 1905 to 1917. Groome was active and participated in the Homestead Strike of 1892 and the Great Strike of 1902. He also served as a colonel in World War I. Groome retired from the police force in 1920.

The Pennsylvania Coal and Iron Police existed from 1865 to 1931 and was also called the Industrial Police. They served the coal companies and the capitalists and oftentimes abused their power against the laboring class. Many of these men were convicted of murder, rape and abuse, but it was kept quiet due to the small size of the coal mine towns where the incidents occurred. Members of the coal and iron police did not care for workers' rights. For this reason, the 1902 Strike Commission Report highly recommended the disbanding of this organization. Governor Pennypacker had hoped the formation of the state police would take the place of the Industrial Police; however, the Pennsylvania coal companies' political ties were too strong to be broken, and both organizations coexisted for twenty-six years before the latter was finally eradicated.

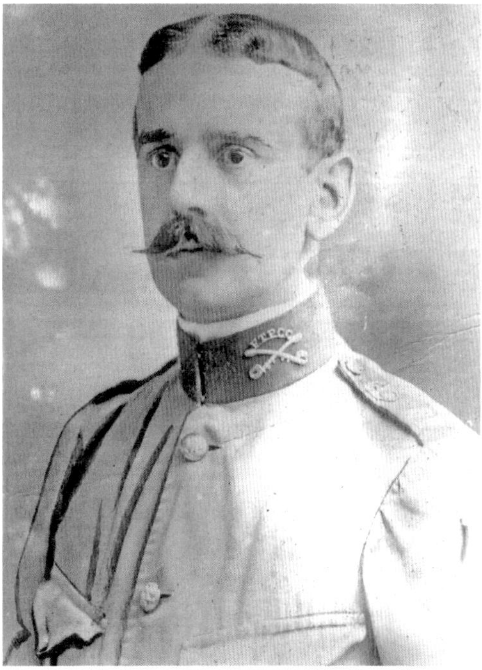

John C. Groome, first commissioner of the Pennsylvania State Police.

FORMATION OF THE THIRTEENTH REGIMENT

Once the Legislation Act of 1878 was passed reorganizing the militia of the state by consolidating the battalions and companies into regiments, it became apparent the end of the Scranton City Guard was near. Permission was granted to raise enough companies locally and have their headquarters located in Scranton. Along with the original Companies A through D, the regiment included Company E (formed in Honesdale), Company F (formed in Carbondale), Company G (formed in Susquehanna) and Company H (formed in Pleasant Valley). In all, eight companies were formed on October 19, 1878, in Scranton. The regiment was mustered in as the Thirteenth Regiment, Third Brigade, National Guard of Pennsylvania.

On August 21, 1879, the Thirteenth Regiment traveled by train to its first encampment in Long Branch, New Jersey. Encampment included guard mounting, picket duty and morning and afternoon drills. Colonel Henry Martyn Boies's report on the encampment impressed the state authorities so much that an encampment of the entire National Guard was scheduled for the following year, and it became an annual event. According to the regiment's historical records, the Thirteenth led the way not only in the organization of encampments but also in rifle practice and competitions.

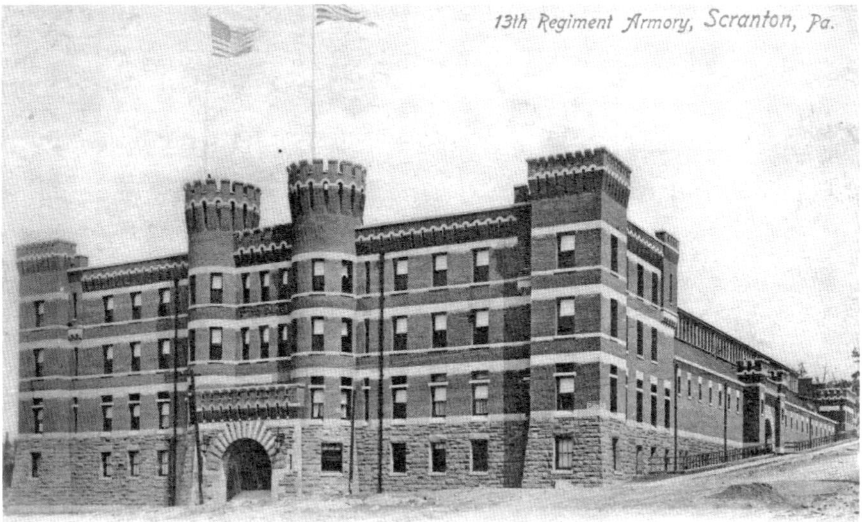

The new home for the Thirteenth Regiment of the Pennsylvania National Guard was erected in 1901; it is better known as the Watres Armory.

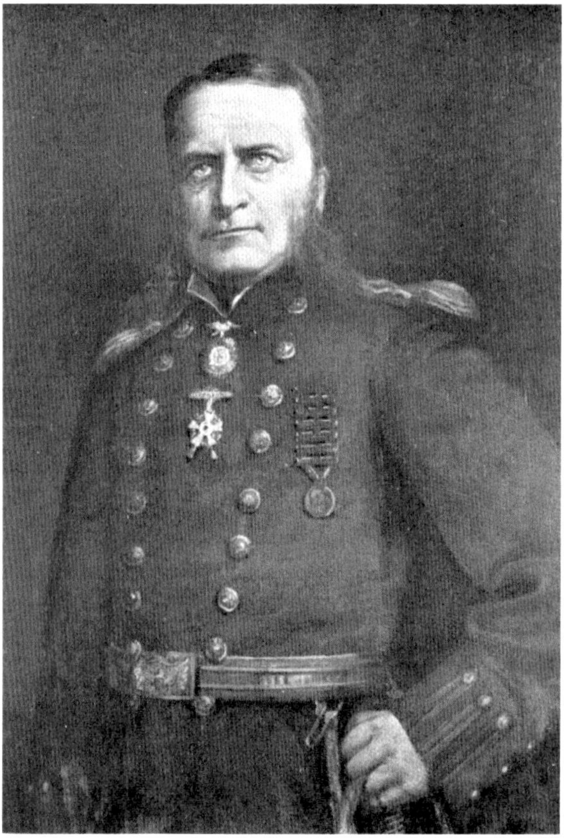

Left: Colonel Henry Martyn Boies, commander of the Scranton City Guard and the Thirteenth Regiment from 1877 to 1883.

Below: The billiard room used for the officers' entertainment in the Thirteenth Regiment Armory.

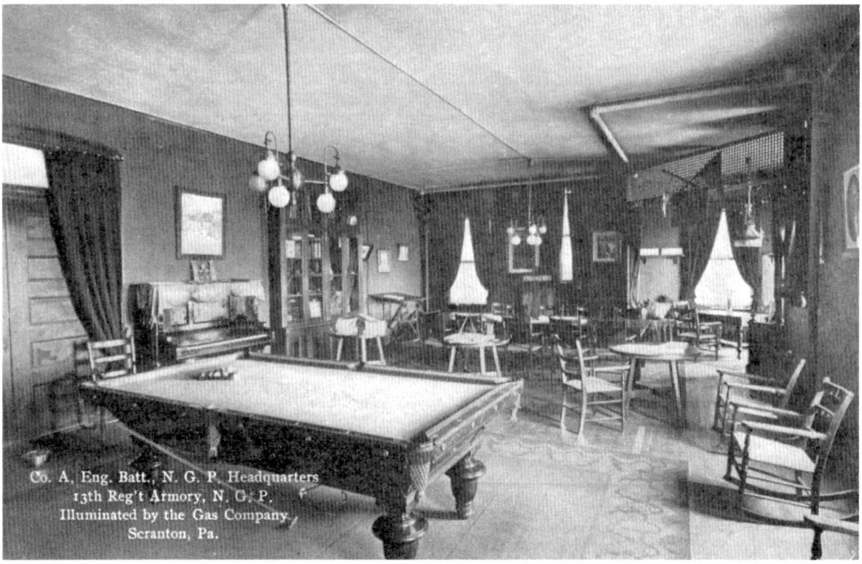

In the spring of 1880, the Thirteenth Regiment held an Armory Fair. In addition to being a financial success, it became known as the social event of the year. Former mayor Robert H. McKune was given the duty of general manager. The entire city took part in the work leading up to the festivities. It is said the armory was transformed into a veritable fairyland, and the women of the city took part in making delicious desserts and running many of the booths. The night air was filled with music and song, and people were treated to other various entertainment. The Armory Fair was held from April 8 to April 17.

In 1899, with the reorganized Thirteenth Regiment on the three-battalion basis, it became evident a larger facility was needed. Colonel Watres offered his help in this matter. The old armory was sold to the Masonic fraternity. After paying off all debts, $30,000 was left that was invested in interest-bearing securities. The new armory was built with monies subscribed independently of the proceeds of the old armory.

A block of land extending from Jefferson Avenue to Adams Avenue, north of Myrtle Street, was purchased in 1899, and construction promptly began. The cornerstone was laid on November 3, 1900. The following brief item is from the *Scranton Times Newspaper*, dated November 3, 1900:

> *The cornerstone of the new Armory was laid by H.M. Boies at 11:30 this morning in the presence of trustees. Mr. Boies pronounced the stone plumed and true. Dr. S.C. Logan offered prayer. There was no military demonstration. A red copper box containing the corner stone of the old armory (laid in 1877) records of the 13th regiment and copies of the daily papers was placed in the corner stone. The following were present, Col. H.M. Boies, Col. F.L. Hitchcock, Col. H.A. Coursen, Lt. Col. C.C. Mattes, Col. Herman Osthauss, and Mayor W.S. Miller.*

Finally, on June 1, 1901, the new armory was completed and opened. The architect was Mr. Lansing C. Holden of New York City, and the contractor was Conrad Shroeder, often called the man who built Scranton.

The red copper box mentioned was discovered and the time capsule opened in 2013.

SAFER WORKING CONDITIONS

The following two men are known both locally and nationally for their efforts to better the working conditions in the mines.

Thomas Jefferson Foster

Thomas Jefferson Foster was a native of Pottsville, Pennsylvania; he is best known as the founder of the International Correspondence School. Prior to that, he worked as an editor for a newspaper in a rural coal mining community. Tragedy hit close to home when a friend of his was killed in a mining accident due to asphyxiation from gas. Believing that the pen was mightier than the sword, Foster wrote several scathing editorials blaming the mining company for its poorly trained foremen, who led the men to their death. Thanks to his editorials and efforts, a law was passed that required safer mine environments. Foster, a former teacher, offered to tutor the miners who had been unable to pass the test the new law required. He developed a course of study for those who were able to attend his classes and for those miners who lived a distance away; they were allowed to mail their answers for Foster to grade. This teaching method led to the formation of the International Correspondence School (ICS) located in Scranton in 1891. The first year's enrollment consisted of 500 miners; a decade later, it reached a staggering 190,000 students. ICS was the first home-study institution of its kind, and by 1906, it offered over five hundred different subjects. The school's motto, "We teach the world," was known around the globe.

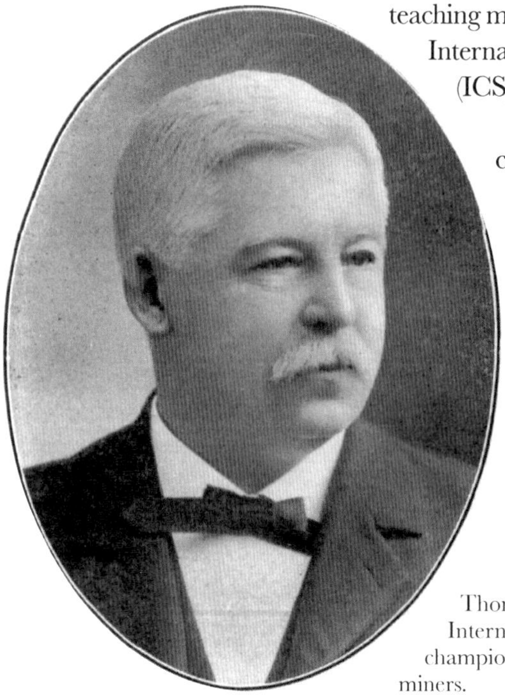

Thomas Jefferson Foster, founder of the International Correspondence School and champion of safer working conditions for coal miners.

Dr. Matthew Shields

At the age of nineteen, Matthew Shields came to Carbondale to practice medicine with his brother, Dr. S.S. Shields. In 1889, he set up his own medical practice not far from Carbondale in Jermyn, Pennsylvania. Inspired by the sound of the breaker whistle signaling when an accident occurred in the mines, Shields made it his mission to help these men. For this reason, in 1899, he organized the original first aid team. Shields taught groups of miners how to stop bleeding by making tourniquets and the general practice of securing broken bones, as well as other simple procedures, in order to assist their fellow workers until medical help arrived. He continued his work in the Jermyn colliery until his house burned down, when he relocated to Scranton. In 1905, Dr. Shields, continuing with his lifesaving work, began to train the employees of the Pennsylvania Coal Company. The following year, he started the annual first aid contests among miners that took place in Scranton and continued for many years.

Dr. Shields's efforts were recognized by the American Red Cross, and he was chosen to teach industrial first aid from 1910 to 1917. During this time, he traveled around the country in one of three special Pullman cars

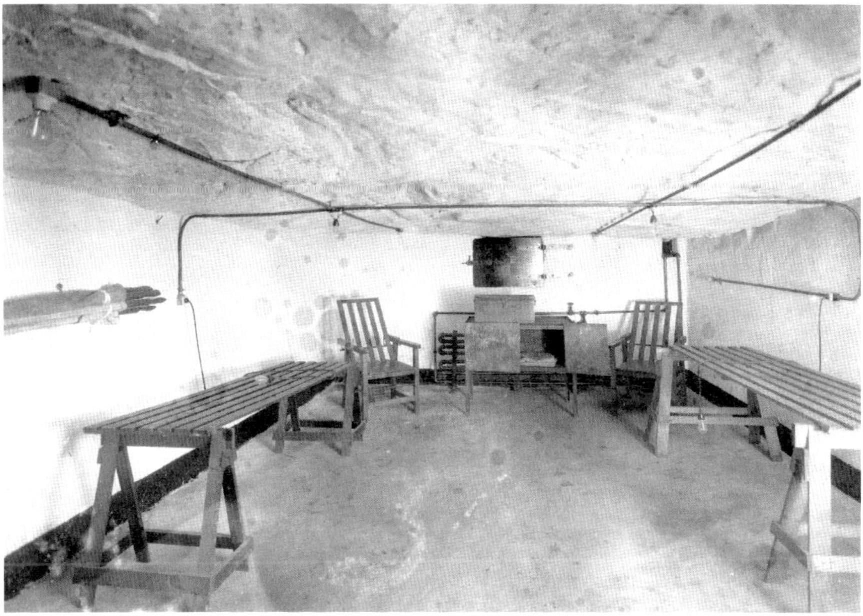

This area was used as a sick bay in the mine.

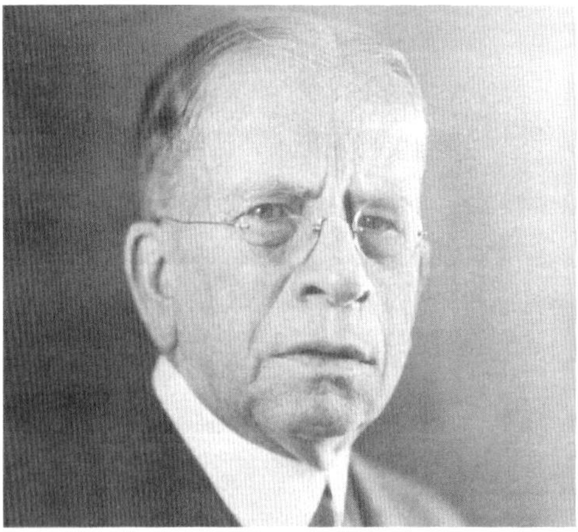

Dr. Matthew Shields, also known as the "Father of Miners' First Aid."

specifically designed for first aid instruction.

Thanks to Dr. Matthew Shields, also known as the "Father of Miners' First Aid," many lives were saved and injuries successfully treated.

OTHER NOTABLE EVENTS IN EARLY LABOR HISTORY

December 28, 1869	Formation of the Knights of Labor under the leadership of Uriah Stephens.
Strike of 1870–71	The strike in the northern field lasted from December 1870 to May 22, 1871, and was often referred to as the "six-month strike." On January 10, 1871, the Workman's Benevolent Association ordered a general strike for the entire region. This strike was disastrous for everyone involved. By the spring of that year, the miners were becoming discontent with the situation, and tempers were starting to get the best of everyone. When several collieries resumed work during the strike, riots began to break out and soldiers were brought in to curb the lawlessness that ran amok in Scranton. But before it was all over, there would be bloodshed. On the sixth of April, a mob became unruly at the Tripps Slope at the end of the workday on Good Friday; a breaker in the Notch section of the city was burned down, and armed strikers and sympathizers took to the streets, beating up workmen who were considered scabs for returning to work during the strike.

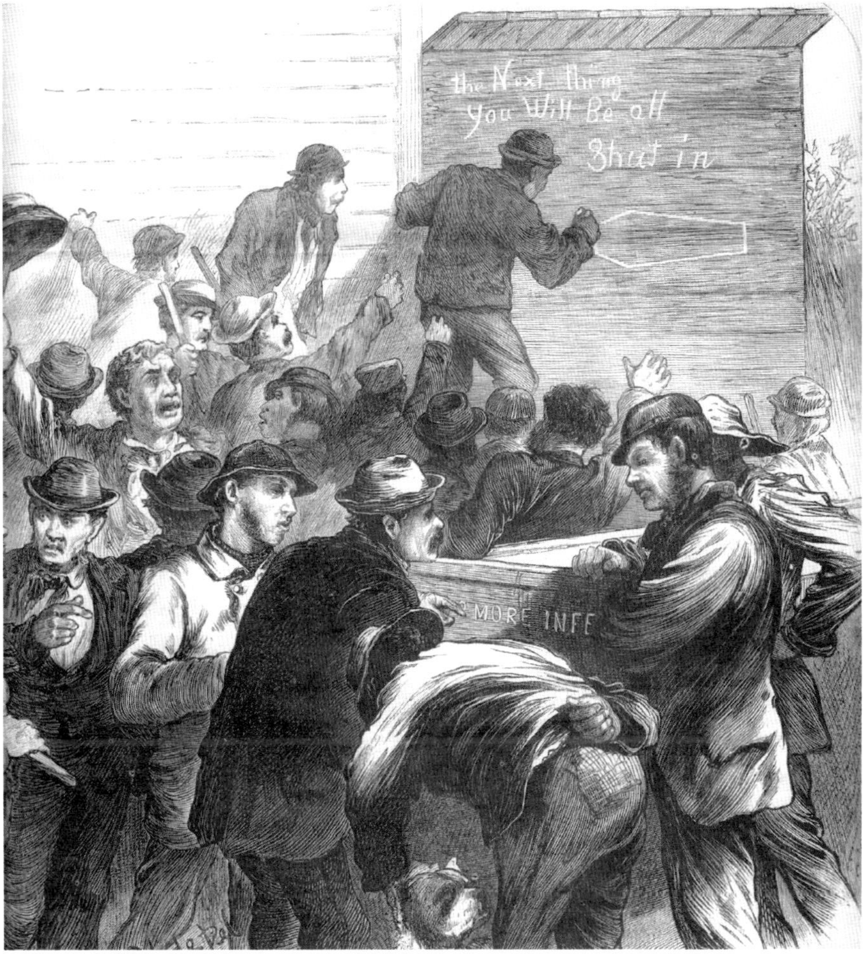

A depiction of the 1870–71 strike in Scranton shows rioters chalking up threats and warnings against "blacklegs" at Church's Mine, near Scranton.

The most violent events occurred late in the day on May 17. A group of thirty or more workers was being escorted home by a company of Zouaves and W.W. Scranton when they were met by a riotous mob of four hundred just east of South Main Avenue and Luzerne Street. Stones and other objects were thrown at the soldiers and miners, and one of the stones hit a Zouave named Cairus. Without warning, the militiamen shot into the crowd, and two men, Benjamin Davis and

	Daniel Jones, fell dead. They were standing behind each other, and the Minié ball from Cairus's rifle went through Davis's body into Jones's. W.W. Scranton ran to the front of the crowd and shouted, "Don't fire, boys. That will do." Many felt that Davis and Jones were both innocent and not involved in the mob, while members of the Zouaves insisted that one of the men shot had thrown the stone that struck Cairus. Five days after the two men were killed, the strike was called off, and on May 28, the militia left the city.
September 5, 1882	Thirty thousand workers marched in the first Labor Day parade in New York City.
May 4, 1886	The Haymarket Riot occurred in Chicago at Haymarket Square when workers rallied together in support of an eight-hour workday. The demonstration took a violent turn when an unknown spectator tossed a bomb and the police fired shots into the crowd. This event gave labor an unsavory reputation and set the movement back for many years.
December 8, 1886	Labor organizer Samuel Gompers set up the American Federation of Labor (AFL). This organization of unions played a key role in the future of the labor movement.
January 25, 1890	United Mine Workers of America is founded.
July 6, 1892	A clash between striking workers at the Homestead Steel Works and Pinkerton detectives hired by the corporation took a violent turn that resulted in the death of seven Pinkertons and eleven union members. The courts ruled in favor of the corporation, thereby breaking up the union. The incident made the steel industry exempt from forming any organized unions for many years.
April 21, 1894 Bituminous Coal Miners' Strike	This unsuccessful two-month strike almost destroyed the United Mine Workers of America.

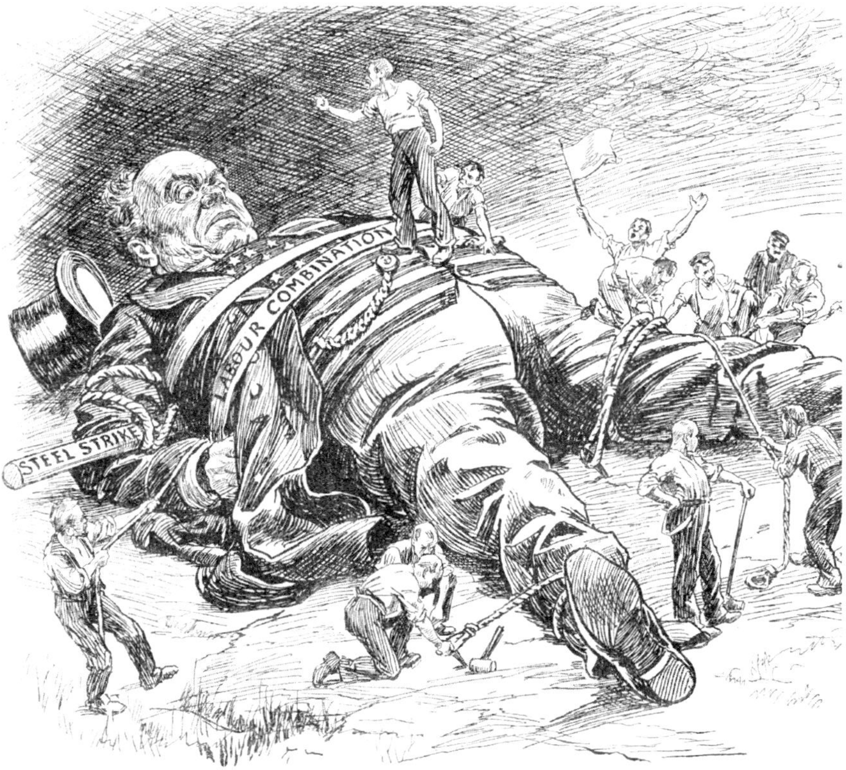

This cartoon depicts the symbol of capitalism during the steel strike.

May 10, 1894	Union workers went on strike at the factory of the Pullman Company located in Illinois. Better known as the "Pullman Strike," it was organized by Eugene V. Debs and the American Railway Union. Labor was defeated.
September 10, 1897 Lattimer Massacre	Once again faced with low wages and poor working conditions, anthracite coal miners of northeastern Pennsylvania went on strike. But poor coal market conditions hardened the operators to the miners' demands, and they decided a show of force by their own company police was needed. On Labor Day, thousands of miners who were supporters of UMWA marched peacefully throughout anthracite mining towns. The UMWA

	leaders urged the marchers to not carry even walking sticks or canes in order to avoid any violent encounters with the iron and coal police. On September 10, the miners marched to Lattimer, where they were stopped by the sheriff of Luzerne County, James Martin. The abrupt encounter turned the peaceful march into one of inexplicable violence. A jostle ensued; shots rang out suddenly, killing nineteen of the miners and wounding fifty more. This horrific event in labor history became known as the Lattimer Massacre. Neither Sheriff Martin nor any members of the coal police were brought up on murder charges despite their hasty, violent actions. As a result of the massacre, there was a rapid growth of unionism in the anthracite coal region, and fifteen thousand new members joined the United Mine Workers of America.
June 27, 1905	Western miners and activists created the Industrial Workers of the World (IWW), also known as the Wobblies. It is considered one of the most radical groups of all the organized unions. The IWW strives to carry on the work of its predecessors as it continues to inspire future generations with its radical spirit.
November 22, 1909	The International Ladies' Garment Workers Union went on strike in New York. It demanded a 20 percent pay raise and a fifty-two-hour workweek. This was the largest labor action by women in labor's history.
May 25, 1911	A fire at the Triangle Shirtwaist Factory located in Manhattan killed 146 female workers due to unsafe working conditions. Reformation was sought to improve working conditions due to the outpour of public sympathy once they learned of the tragic event.
January 12, 1912 Bread and Roses Strike	Workers at the American Woolen Company in Massachusetts took to the picket line due to wage cuts. The strike became a history-making confrontation between labor and capital.

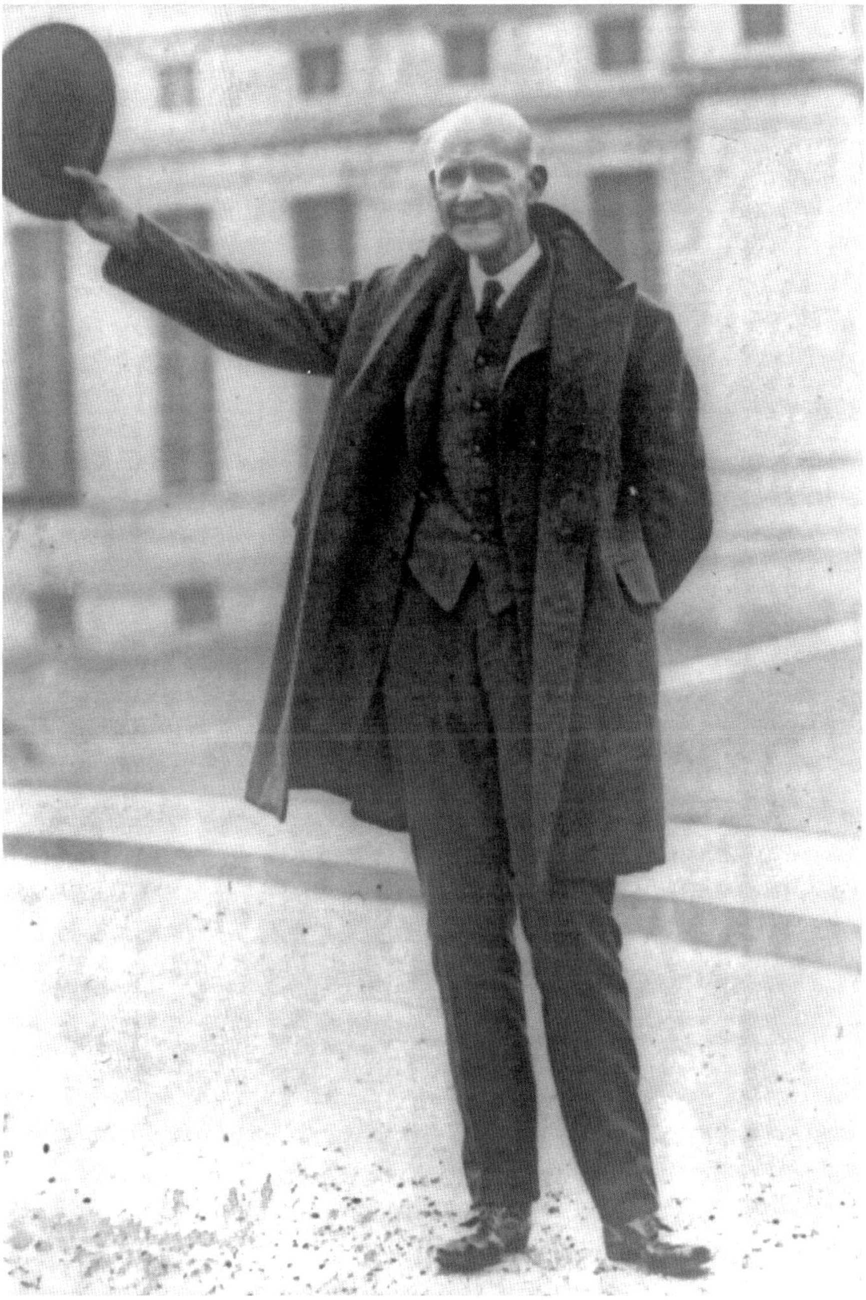

Eugene V. Debs, American union leader and one of the founders of the Industrial Workers of the World.

June 12, 1912	The first state minimum-wage law was adopted in Massachusetts, which gave women and children wage security. Other states passed similar laws during the same year.
March 4, 1913	The Federal Department of Labor was founded. This department was established under President Taft; he signed the law after he was defeated in the 1912 election.
November 19, 1915	Industrial Workers of the World union member and songwriter Joe Hill was executed in Utah after being convicted of murder. Due to his songs and the well-publicized call to his fellow workers on the eve of his execution, "Don't waste time mourning, organize!" Hill became the best-known IWW martyr and labor folk hero.
June 25, 1938	After many years of blood, sweat and tears, a milestone was finally made on this date when the Fair Labor Standards Act was established. This act set a standard-hour workweek with time and a half for additional hours. It also put severe restrictions on child labor and established a national minimum wage.

IN THE END

Here in Scranton, the "Great Strike" left a legacy that remains of great importance to this day. On Memorial Day 1924, a monument was dedicated to John Mitchell. It consists of three sections. The first is a lifelike bronze statue of John Mitchell. The second is a carved scene of six miners at work, a mule pulling a car of coal and a driver boy. The third, which is located at the rear of the monument, shows the miner at home with his family. The memorial to the labor leader is located at the Lackawanna County Courthouse in Scranton, where the Anthracite Coal Strike Commission hearings began in November 1902. Every year, people gather around the statue to celebrate "John Mitchell Day," October 29, in remembrance of Mitchell's success in the coal strike of 1900.

In August 2008, a Pennsylvania Historical and Museum Commission historical marker was dedicated at the intersection of Lackawanna and

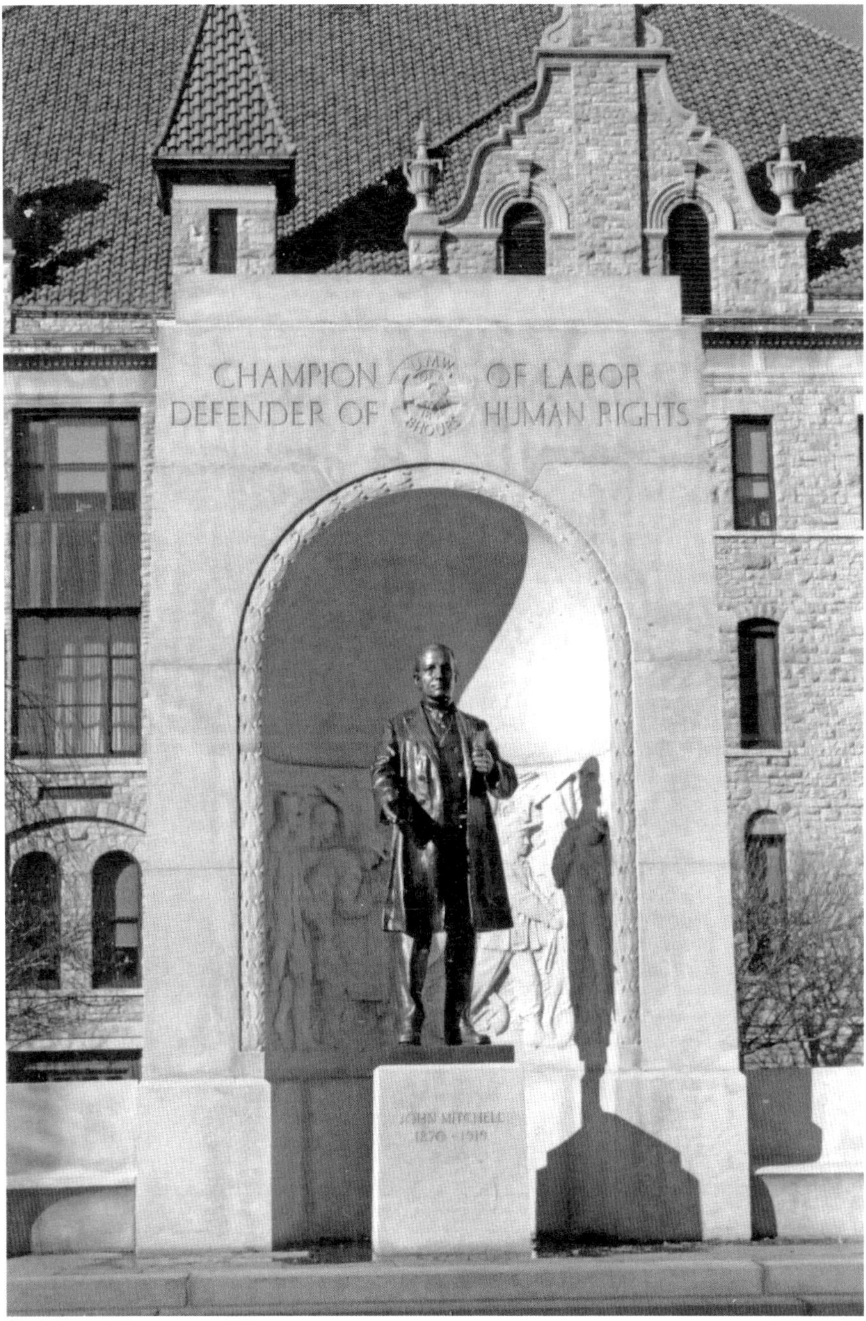

The Johnny Mitchell Monument is located in Scranton at Courthhouse Square; it was dedicated in 1924, and people gather annually in honor of Johnny Mitchell Day every October 29.

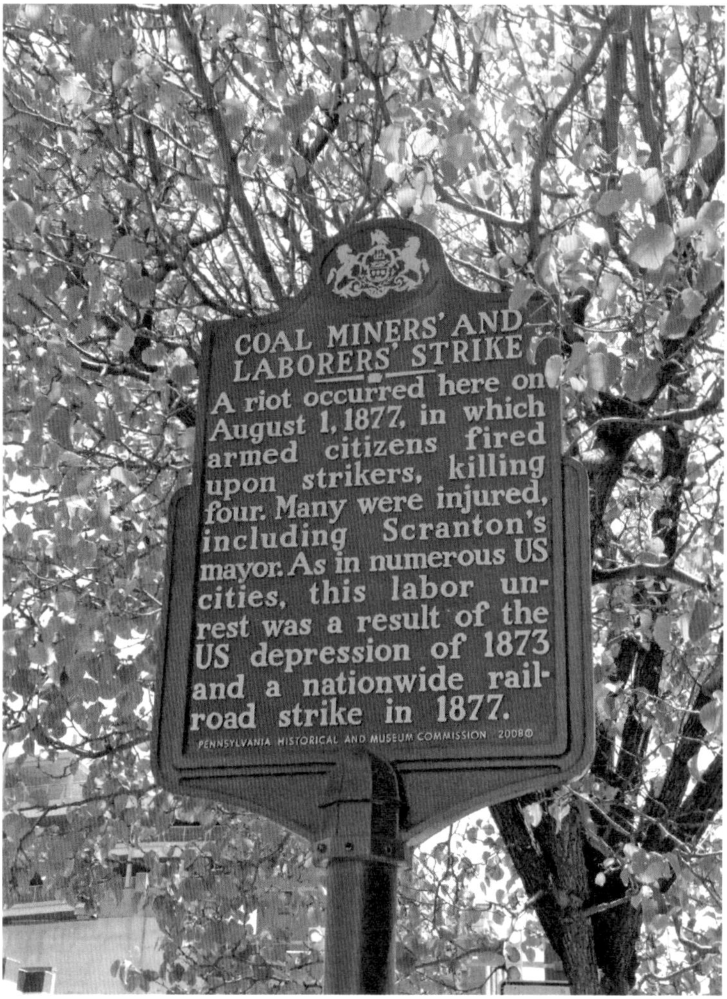

The Pennsylvania Historical and Museum Commission Marker was dedicated in August 2008 in honor of the coal miners' and laborers' strike of 1877. The marker is located on the 400 block of Lackawanna Avenue.

Washington Avenues in honor of the Coal Miners' and Laborers' Strike of 1877. It reads: "A riot occurred here on August 1, 1877, in which armed citizens fired upon strikers, killing four. Many were injured, including Scranton's mayor. As in numerous U.S. cities, this labor unrest was a result of the U.S. depression of 1873 and a nationwide railroad strike in 1877."

Both symbols are a reminder to all of the importance Scranton, Pennsylvania, played in the nation's labor movement.

Bibliography

Books

Bruce, Robert V. *1877: Year of Violence*. Chicago: Quadrangle Paperbacks, 1970.

Craft, David, William A. Wilcox, Alfred Hand and J. Wooldridge. *History of Scranton, Penn. With Full Outline of the Natural Advantages, Accounts of the Indian Tribes, Early Settlements, Connecticut's Claim to the Wyoming Valley, the Trenton Decree, Manufacturing, Mining, and Transportation Interests, the Press, Churches, Societies, Etc., Etc., Down to the Present Time.* Dayton, OH: United Brethren Publishing House, 1891.

Dailey, Lucia. *Mine Seed*. Bloomington, IN: Lucia Daily, 2002.

Gibbons, Phoebe E. "The Miners of Scranton." In *Harper's New Monthly Magazine Volume LV. June to November, 1877*. New York: Harper & Brothers, 1877, 916–27.

Hitchcock, Frederick L. *History of Scranton and Its People*. Vols. 1 and 2. New York: Lewis Historical Publishing Company, 1914.

Hollister, H. *History of the Lackawanna Valley*. 6th ed. Scranton, PA: Tribune Publishing Company, 1903.

Janosov, Robert A. "Beyond 'The Great Coal Strike': The Anthracite Region in 1902." In *The "Great Strike": Perspectives on the 1902 Anthracite Coal Strike*. Easton, PA: Canal History and Technology Press, 2002, 1–28.

Jones, Mary Harris. *Autobiography of Mother Jones*. Mineola, NY: Dover Publications, 2004.

Lears, Jackson. *Rebirth of a Nation: The Making of Modern America, 1877–1920*. New York: HarperCollins, 2009.

Levy, Elizabeth, and Tad Richards. *Struggle and Lose, Struggle and Win: The United Mine Workers*. New York: Four Winds Press, 1977.

Logan, Samuel C. *A City's Danger and Defense; or, Issues and Results of the Strikes of 1877, Containing the Origin and History of the Scranton City Guard*. Scranton, PA: Samuel C. Logan, DD, 1887.

McKerns, Joseph P. "The 'Faces' of John Mitchell: News Coverage of the Great Anthracite Strike of 1902 in the Regional and National Press." In *The "Great Strike": Perspectives on the 1902 Anthracite Coal Strike*. Easton, PA: Canal History and Technology Press, 2002, 29–42.

McKune, Robert H. *Memorial of the Erection of Lackawanna County, in the State of Pennsylvania: Comprising an Account of the Progress of the New-County Movement, the Laying of the Corner-Stone of the Court-House and a Stenographic Report of the Speeches at the Banquet Held*. Cranberry Township, PA: Bookkeeper Preservation Technologies Inc., 1997.

Metz, Lance E. "The Role of Intimidation and Violence in the Great Anthracite Strike of 1902." In *The "Great Strike": Perspectives on the 1902 Anthracite Coal Strike*. Easton, PA: Canal History and Technology Press, 2002, 43–66.

Murphy, Thomas. *History of Lackawanna County, Pennsylvania*. Vols. 1 and 2. Indianapolis, IN: Historical Publishing Company, 1928.

Richards, J. Stuart. *Death in the Mines: Disasters and Rescues in the Anthracite Coal Fields of Pennsylvania*. Charleston, SC: The History Press, 2007.

Sadler, Spencer J. *Pennsylvania's Coal and Iron Police.* Charleston, SC: Arcadia Publishing, 2009.

Weinberg, Arthur, ed. *Attorney for the Damned: Clarence Darrow in the Courtroom.* Chicago: University of Chicago Press, 1989.

Wenzel, David J. *Scranton's Mayors.* Eynon, PA: Tribute Books, 2006.

ARTICLES

Citizens Voice. "Army Protected Local Collieries During Railroad Strike of 1877." May 13, 2008.

Scranton Times. "Armory." November 3, 1900.

Stanislaus, Richard. "John Mitchell Monument." *Miner's Lamp* 9, no. 5 (1992): 1.

PRESENTATIONS

Azzarelli, Margo. *1877: Riot on Lackawanna Avenue.* Theatrical production. Lackawanna Iron Furnaces, 2007.

WEBSITES AND ONLINE RESOURCES

AFLCIO. "Labor History Timeline" http://www.aflcio.org/About/Our-History/Labor-History-Timeline.

American Red Cross. "Our History." http://www.redcross.org/about-us/history.

Andrews, Thomas G. "Coal and the Industrial Revolution." *Teaching History.* http://teachinghistory.org/historycontent/beyond-the-textbook/23923.

Connelly, Scott. "The Greatest Strike Ever." Penn State University. Spring 2010. http://pabook2.libraries.psu.edu/palitmap/Coal1902.html.

ExplorePAhistory. "Mining Anthracite." http://explorepahistory.com/story.php?storyId=1-9-B. FemBio.

———. "The 1902 Anthracite Coal Strike (Scranton) Historical Marker." http://explorepahistory.com/hmarker.php?markerId=1-A-B7.

Grossman, Jonathan. "The Coal Strike of 1902—Turning Point in U.S. Policy." *United States Department of Labor*. http://www.dol.gov/dol/aboutdol/history/coalstrike.htm.

Industrial Workers of the World. "Chronology of IWW History." http://www.iww.org/history/chronology.

Kheel Staff. "Guide to the John Mitchell Papers on Microfilm." Cornell University. http://rmc.library.cornell.edu/EAD/htmldocs/KCL05502mf.html.

Lyricsmode. "Sixteen Tons Lyrics." http://www.lyricsmode.com/lyrics/t/tennessee_ernie_ford/sixteen_tons.html.

Manning, Joseph H. "Joseph Puma." Mornings on Maple Street. http://www.morningsonmaplestreet.com/josephpuma1.html.

"Mary Harris Jones (Mother Jones)." http://www.fembio.org/english/biography.php/woman/biography/mary-harris-mother-jones/.

McDowell, John. "The Slow Progress of the Boy Who Starts in a Breaker, and Ends, an Old Man in the Breaker—As Told by a Man Who Was Once a Miner." *The World's Work* 4 (October 1902). https://ehistory.osu.edu/exhibitions/gildedage/content/LifeofaCoalMiner.

Mountjoy, Eileen. "A Woman's Day: Work and Anxiety." Indiana University of Pennsylvania. http://www.iup.edu/archives/coal/people-lives-stories/a-woman-s-day--work-and-anxiety/.

The National Museum of American History. "Mining Lights and Hats." http://americanhistory.si.edu/collections/object-groups/mining-lights-and-hats.

Pennsylvania State Police. "Pennsylvania State Police History." http://psp-hemc.org/history/psp.html.

PSEA. "Labor History in America." http://psea.org/labor.

Schmoop. "History of Labor Unions Timeline." http://www.shmoop.com/history-labor-unions/timeline.html.

Scranton Republican. "Labor's Great Part in Progress of City; Great Leaders." Ancestry.com. http://homepages.rootsweb.ancestry.com/~alaine/history/newspaper/labor.html.

Steamtown. "Delaware, Lackawanna & Western Railroad No. 565." http://www.nps.gov/parkhistory/online_books/steamtown/shs2f.htm.

UMWA. "Health and Safety on the Job: Black Lung." http://www.umwa.org/?q=content/black-lung.

United States Department of Labor. "A Pictorial Walk Through the 20th Century." http://www.msha.gov/CENTURY/CANARY/CANARY.asp.

West, Bob. "America's Oldest Division Celebrates Its 120th Birthday." http://www.bob-west.com/1B-28th.html.

INDEX

A

American Federation of Labor 71, 88, 122
American Red Cross 63, 119
anthracite coal 13, 47, 48, 49, 83, 86, 87, 90, 91, 92, 101, 123
Arnot, Pennsylvania 80
Avondale mine disaster 56

B

Baer, George F. 90, 91, 109
bituminous coal 13, 48, 82
black damp 55
black lung disease 58
Black Maria 61
Boies, Henry Martyn 37, 73, 115
breaker boys 58
Brotherhood of Railway-men 19
Brotherhood of Trainmen 23

C

canaries 56
Civil War 11, 13, 19, 23, 47, 69, 72, 74, 75
company store 28, 54, 63, 64
Cooke, Jay 13

D

Darrow, Clarence 12, 76, 81, 109
Debs, Eugene V. 76, 123
Delaware, Lackawanna and Western Railroad 17, 19, 26, 48, 71

E

Edwardian era 86

F

Federal Department of Labor 126
fire damp 55, 58
First Presbyterian Church 27, 42, 70
Foster, Thomas Jefferson 118

G

German immigrants 65, 66, 67
Gibbons, Phoebe 65
Great Strike of 1902 81, 88, 108, 111, 114
Groome, John Charles 114

H

Harding, Judge Garrick M. 36
Hartranft, Governor John 15, 32
Haymarket Riot 76, 122
Hill, Joe 126
Homestead Steel Works 122

I

Industrial Revolution 11, 47, 85
Industrial Workers of the World 126
International Ladies' Garment Workers Union 124
Irish immigrants 49, 65, 66, 67, 80, 90
Italian immigrants 66, 94

J

Jones, Mother 78, 83, 90, 91, 92, 109, 110

K

Klondike colliery 100
Knights of Labor 71, 72, 80, 82, 88, 120

L

la Belle Époque 86, 88
laborers 19, 24, 36, 49, 51, 56, 80, 81, 91, 102, 103, 107
Lackawanna Avenue 22, 29, 32, 46
Lackawanna County 46
Lackawanna County Courthouse 12, 76, 109
Lackawanna Iron and Coal Company 72, 73
Lattimer Massacre 110, 124
Logan, Samuel C. 38, 42, 70
Luzerne County 46, 124

M

McDowell, Reverend John 51
McKinley, William 72, 90
McKune, Robert H. 15, 69, 117
Miners Association 35
Mitchell, John 12, 81, 82, 90, 93, 101, 102, 109, 126
Morgan, J.P. 91, 107
mule boy 51, 58

N

National Civic Federation 92
nipper 51, 58

P

Pennsylvania Coal and Iron Police 93, 114
Pennsylvania National Guard 74, 100
Pennsylvania Railroad 14
Pennsylvania State Police 113, 114
Pinkerton detectives 75, 122
Pittsburgh 15, 75
Polish immigrants 90
Powderly, Terence 45, 70, 72
pre–World War I era 86
Progressive era 88, 105
Pullman Strike 76, 123

R

railroad brotherhoods 15
riot on Lackawanna Avenue 110
riots of 1877 12, 71
Ripple, Ezra 24, 33, 75
Roosevelt, Theodore 12, 75, 81, 100, 102, 113
Root, Elihu 107
Roundwoods 19, 24, 25, 43

S

scabs 80, 93, 120
Scranton Citizens' Corps 22
Scranton City Guard 37, 42, 43, 71, 74, 76, 115
Scranton, W.W. 22, 23, 24, 29, 32, 33, 35, 121, 122
Shenandoah 98
Shields, Matthew 63, 119

silk mills 78, 81
silkworks 24
Snow, Phoebe 48, 86

T

Thirteenth Regiment 43, 74, 75, 76, 115, 117
Triangle Shirtwaist Factory 124

U

United Mine Workers of America 80, 82, 89, 90, 122, 124

W

Welsh immigrants 49, 65, 66, 67, 94
white damp 55
Workers Benevolent Association 88
Wright, Carroll D. 101

About the Authors

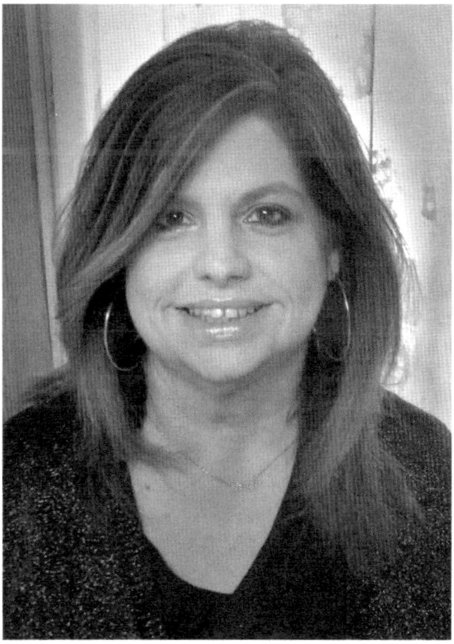

Margo L. Azzarelli lives in Scranton, Pennsylvania, with her husband, Dominick; her daughter, Marnie; and three fur babies. Her love for writing began at the age of twelve, after reading her first Gothic Romance novel.

Azzarelli is a historian/researcher who has written four local history books for Arcadia/The History Press and is the local history columnist for "Our Town, Lackawanna County."

A charter member of the Triboro Historical Society, she currently serves on the board as second vice-president and volunteers her time to several community historical societies.

Marnie Azzarelli is a local historian and docent for the Lackawanna Historical Society. In 2014, she graduated from Marywood University with a bachelor's degree in English and received the J. Harold Brislin Award for distinction in creative writing. Her short fiction has been published in Marywood's literary publication *The Bayleaf* and a literary magazine called *Clever Girl*. When not writing about the rights of the workingman, Marnie reviews TV shows online, writes horror stories that only scare herself and wears hoopskirts for fun. She lives with her two cats, one puppy and two parents in Scranton, Pennsylvania.

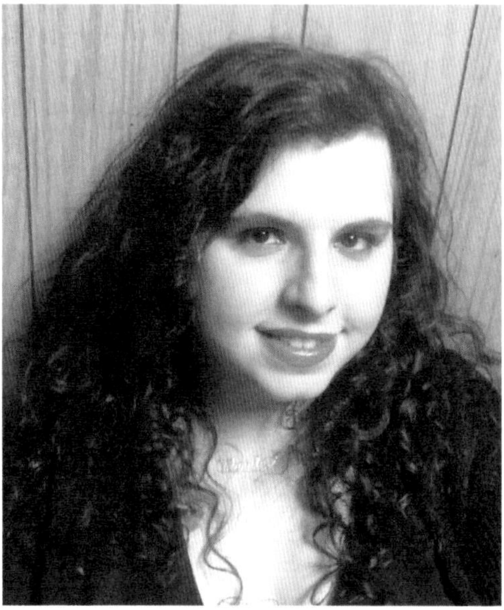

Visit us at
www.historypress.net

This title is also available as an e-book